BUILDING A BETTER SOCIETY

Liverpool's historic institutional buildings

Published by English Heritage, Kemble Drive, Swindon SN2 2GZ
www.english-heritage.org.uk
English Heritage is the Government's statutory adviser on all aspects of the historic environment.

Printing 10 9 8 7 6 5 4 3 2 1

First published 2008

ISBN 978 1 873592 90 8
Product code 51332

The Charity Commission has made a financial contribution towards the publication of this book.

British Library Cataloguing in Publication Data
A CIP catalogue record for this book is available from the British Library.

The National Monuments Record is the public archive of English Heritage. For more information, contact NMR Enquiry and Research Services, National Monuments Record Centre, Kemble Drive, Swindon SN2 2GZ; telephone (01793) 414600.

Brought to publication by Rachel Howard and René Rodgers, Publishing, English Heritage.
Edited by Sara Peacock.
Page layout by Simon Borrough.
Printed in UK by Cambridge Printing.

Front cover
Mechanics' Institution (Liverpool Institute for Performing Arts).
[DP039472]

Inside front cover
Everton Library, St Domingo Road (1896, Thomas Shelmerdine).
[DP039344]

Back cover
Headstone recording deaths at the Liverpool Orphan Boys' Asylum, St James' Cemetery, below the Anglican Cathedral. [DPO39471]

BUILDING A BETTER SOCIETY

Liverpool's historic institutional buildings

Colum Giles

CHARITY COMMISSION

The City of Liverpool

Liverpool
EUROPEAN
CAPITAL OF CULTURE

ENGLISH HERITAGE

Contents

Frontispiece
Street urchins awaiting a Christmas feast in St George's Hall. [Liverpool Record Office, Liverpool Libraries, from Birt 1913]

Acknowledgements

Many people have given valuable help in bringing this book to publication. English Heritage colleagues, in particular Ian Goodall, Henry Owen-John, Peter de Figueiredo and Louise O'Brien, but also John Stonard, John Cattell, Adam Menuge, Matthew Withey, Simon Taylor, Garry Corbett and Paul Barnwell, provided advice and support. Peter Williams, Tony Perry, Bob Skingle and Keith Buck took the photographs, Allan Adams produced the maps and drawn illustrations, and Kate Bould and Ursula Dugard Craig provided administrative support. Colleagues in the National Monuments Record, in particular Nigel Wilkins, helped to identify and produce illustrations, and design and production were co-ordinated by Rachel Howard and Dr Robin Taylor. The text has benefited from the comments of a number of readers, including Dr Pat Starkey, Professor Robert Lee and Sarah Pearson, and Joseph Sharples provided advice and made available his extensive knowledge of Liverpool buildings. Kate McNichol at the Merseyside Police Information Management Department, Alistair Sunderland and Karen Monks of Austin-Smith: Lord LLP, and staff at Liverpool Record Office, in particular Roger Hull, were an immense help in making archives and illustrative material available. English Heritage has gained from the support of the Charity Commission through the help of Nick Allaway, Neville Brownlee and Christina Clarke, and it has been a pleasure to share the objective of making a contribution to Liverpool's cultural life through the production of this book. English Heritage's long-term partnership with Liverpool City Council, through the Historic Environment of Liverpool Project, has involved the help and support of Council officers, principally Nigel Lee. Finally, acknowledgement should be made to the owners and occupiers of the institutional buildings which form the subject of this book. Their continued care will help to ensure that an important aspect of Liverpool's social, cultural and architectural history can be enjoyed by a wide public.

Dedication

This book is dedicated to the memory of Ian Goodall (1948–2006), late Senior Investigator with English Heritage, who undertook much of the research for it. His commitment to the project ensured that this important aspect of Liverpool's historic environment received the recognition it deserves.

Foreword

Today's universal education, health and benefit systems were developed slowly by local government in the course of the 19th and 20th centuries. Before they became fully effective, charity, philanthropy and private donations were the principal means of helping the needy. This book tells the story of how charitable effort, later combined with an increasing involvement by the state, addressed the social issues raised by the massive growth of Liverpool in the 19th century, and it does this through the institutional buildings which form such an important part of the city's landscape.

English Heritage and Liverpool City Council have been supported in this project by the Charity Commission, which has one of its major regional offices in the city. Liverpool continues to have a dynamic and innovative charitable sector and the Commission supports the important role that charities play in the life of the city. Many of the charities responsible for the buildings illustrated in this book continue to be active in the city and beyond. The Commission is keen to promote an understanding of the importance of charitable effort in Liverpool and recognises that this can be celebrated through a discovery of the buildings constructed to carry out charitable work. The care of this legacy is officially the concern of English Heritage and of Liverpool City Council, but in fact the people of Liverpool – as owners, occupiers, developers or simply citizens – share in this role. It is hoped that better understanding of these buildings – what inspired their construction, what services they provided, what part they played in ordinary people's lives – will lead to greater appreciation of how they contribute to Liverpool's distinctive culture and landscapes. The story is, in part, a reminder of harsher days, but it also demonstrates how Liverpool's people responded to desperate need. The work of charitable institutions is still important here today: this book provides the historical background to the continuing effort to improve people's lives.

Lord Bruce-Lockhart, Chairman, English Heritage
Councillor Warren Bradley, Leader, Liverpool City Council
Dame Suzi Leather, Chair, Charity Commission

CHAPTER 1

Introduction

In the centre of Liverpool, just below the monumental St George's Hall, lie St John's Gardens. Attractively laid out early in the 20th century, and now with mature trees around their perimeter, the gardens offer a much-needed green open space in the busy city (Fig 1). However, the features of the gardens, and the views from them, have another significance, telling the story of how Liverpool both exploited the opportunities offered by its meteoric rise in the 18th and 19th centuries and at the same time devised responses to some of the immense social problems which accompanied that growth.

The views from the Gardens are dominated by imposing buildings, most of them demonstrating the cultural achievements of the second half of the 19th century. St George's Hall began in 1836 as a scheme which invited public subscriptions to build a hall for musical performances and large meetings, a facility which the town previously lacked. Its construction caused the demolition of the Seamen's Hospital and the Infirmary, two of the principal charitable institutions of the 18th century. To the north lie the buildings of William Brown Street, a hugely

Figure 1 (right) *St John's Gardens, below St George's Hall, opened in 1904. They were designed by Liverpool Corporation's Surveyor, Thomas Shelmerdine.* [DP039369]

Detail of the statue of Monsignor James Nugent. [DP045347]

impressive Classical stage set produced by civic pride and philanthropic zeal (Fig 2). In the centre is the William Brown Library and Museum (1857–60), originally the Liverpool Free Public Library, funded by the merchant and banker whose name it took. Next to it, on the uphill side, is the massive domed drum of the Picton Reading Room (1875–9), commemorating one of the most prominent scholars in the city in the 19th century. Uphill again is the Walker Art Gallery (1874–7), a gift to the city from the brewer Andrew Barclay Walker. Topping and tailing the group are the County Sessions House (1882–4) and the Technical School, now the World Museum, Liverpool. The buildings tell a story of developing urban self-awareness, wealth and confidence.

Figure 2 *Civic pride funded by charitable donation: William Brown Street. In the centre is the Walker Art Gallery (1874–7, Sherlock and Vale), and downhill from it are, first, the circular Picton Reading Room (1875–9, Cornelius Sherlock), and the William Brown Library and Museum (1857–60, John Weightman). [AA045129]*

Figure 3 *Sectarian unity of purpose: statues of* (right) *Monsignor James Nugent (1905) and* (far right) *Canon Major Lester (1907), leaders in the provision of education and shelter for poor children. [DP039372, DP039373]*

The Gardens themselves continue this theme, for arranged around the open area are statues of the eminent and powerful in Liverpool's rise to greatness. Right in the centre is the city's most celebrated son, William Ewart Gladstone, four times Prime Minister, born in Rodney Street less than a mile away. Behind and to either side are statues of William Rathbone, Sir Arthur Bower Forwood and Alexander Balfour, all important figures in the life of the city and all deriving fortunes from trade and shipping. But while Forwood devoted his energies to accumulating wealth and political power, Rathbone and Balfour provide a link to another face of 19th-century Liverpool, for both were active in charitable work and in efforts to relieve distress. Rathbone was central to the debate about the role of charity which rumbled through the decades as Liverpool struggled to come to terms with contemporary urban problems, and Balfour did much for the temperance movement and to help seamen. Finally, a little below these great figures, are two more statues, one of Monsignor James Nugent (1822–1905), a Roman Catholic priest, the other of Major Lester (1829–1903), an Anglican canon (Fig 3). Both are portrayed with a small child, representing the poor children of the city whom they did so much to help through charitable work. They could hardly be further apart within St John's Gardens, but this seems to have been the result of a desire for balance within the open space rather than an unconscious reflection of the sectarian divide which was so powerful in Liverpool in the 19th century. Despite their different creeds, both used their zeal and commitment to prick consciences and raise awareness of the squalor – moral, spiritual and physical – which characterised the life of Liverpool's underclass.

The views from St John's Gardens, therefore, offer an insight into two sides of Liverpool's life in the 19th century. One is about corporate and political achievement, the other tells the story, equally impressive but today less recognised, of the struggle to deal with the city's growing pains. It is this difficult story, one which continues to the present day, which forms the main subject of this book.

Although charitable institutions were important in the life of Liverpool in the 18th century, the focus of this book is on the 19th century. This was when the need was at its greatest and when charitable effort provided the only hope of an adequate response. This book is primarily about the legacy of institutional life in Liverpool. Institutional buildings are often fine architecture, but this book does not set out to provide a detailed study of the development of building types. Instead, it focuses on the way that institutional buildings tell us about almost forgotten aspects of a traumatic – because so rapidly changing – period in the city's history. They demonstrate the impact which institutions made on the newly forming urban landscape, and they also reveal a great deal about the hopes, fears and attitudes of the participants, both benefactors and recipients of charity. This book tells the story of Liverpool's institutional buildings by showing how the poor and disadvantaged encountered institutions in their everyday lives. A second theme – the distribution of institutions across the city and through time – cuts across this story. Some institutions, particularly those purporting to serve the whole city, are clustered in the centre, some in a very conspicuous 'institutional quarter'. Others began in the centre and relocated to more spacious surroundings on the outskirts. And others were always designed to address purely local needs, and are scattered widely across the whole city. Their impact on suburban Liverpool will be assessed by taking one small area – Kirkdale, in the north of the city – for special attention. The buildings which served local communities are less well known than the sometimes grand central institutions, but each played a part in constructing a new society.

CHAPTER 2

Government
and charity in
19th-century Liverpool

King John granted a letters patent making Liverpool a borough in 1207, but for centuries it was little more than a village beside a castle. The village became a thriving port by the 17th century and the leading port outside London by the early 19th century. The growth of the town – with a population rising from about 6,000 in 1700 to 165,000 in 1831 and, helped in part by boundary extensions, to over half a million in 1891 – matched its commercial achievements. Originally a simple chapelry within Walton parish, the town – a city after 1880 – absorbed the outlying townships and dominated a conurbation which ultimately stretched from Speke in the south to Crosby in the north.

In Britain today, most people accept that essential services such as health care, education and social welfare are public responsibilities, to be provided by local or national government and paid for out of taxation. However, this state of affairs came about only gradually during the course of the 19th and 20th centuries. In the early Victorian period, when the acute social problems caused by rapid industrialisation and urbanisation were first being faced, there was no such consensus, and in any case local government lacked the statutory powers to make such provision. The prevailing liberal doctrine of 'laissez-faire' allowed a very limited role for the state in the regulation of society and the economy, and this applied at both national and local levels. While this might have been adequate in earlier days, it was not capable of dealing effectively with the wholly new circumstances created by rapid expansion.

The challenge of a new society

In Liverpool, growth brought with it a crisis in living conditions for the poor. Extreme overcrowding, disease, appalling housing, and inadequate sanitary provision were the lot of thousands of inhabitants throughout this period. Before the mid-19th century, the Corporation acted as far as its limited powers allowed, attempting to cleanse and light the streets and, in *c*1770, constructing a large workhouse on Brownlow Hill. This loomed above the expanding town and grew into one of the largest workhouses in the country, in a harsh age acting as a solemn reminder of the

Christ healing the blind; carved detail on the former Eye and Ear Infirmary, Myrtle Street (1878–80). [DP039404]

consequences of failure in the survival game (Fig 4). The reality of the urban crisis in the wake of epidemics of cholera and typhus at last prompted change in the 1840s: the Liverpool Sanitary Act of 1846 enabled the Corporation to appoint a Medical Officer of Health, and at a national level the 1848 Public Health Act permitted local authorities to improve sanitation, housing standards, water supplies and sewerage.

Liverpool was not alone in facing these problems, but the view emerged that it was here that the urban crisis was felt most deeply. Already by the early 19th century, Liverpool had become notorious for its social problems: it was said to be 'infested with beggars from the adjacent country', and prostitution was seen as so widespread as to pose a threat to society.[1] In 1840 Dr William Duncan pronounced Liverpool to be the 'unhealthiest town in England'.[2] On being appointed as Medical

Figure 4 *Liverpool Workhouse on Brownlow Hill: a town within a town, with over 5,000 inmates by the early 20th century. It was demolished in the 1930s to make way for the Roman Catholic Cathedral. [Liverpool Record Office, Liverpool Libraries, Photographs and Small Prints]*

Officer of Health in 1846 (the first such post in the country), Duncan set about demonstrating the connection between living conditions in narrow courts and cellars, for which Liverpool was notorious, the incidence of cholera and typhus, and the appalling mortality rates in the most overcrowded areas of the city.

It may be that Liverpool did indeed suffer more than other places, since there were special circumstances here which made the consequences of demographic growth much more serious. First, although its rise made it seem like a boom town, its docks and warehouses offered only insecure casual employment for unskilled labourers, and the bright hopes of many newcomers must soon have been dashed as they struggled to make a living. Second, its growing importance as a port made it a focus for migration, from the north and midlands of England, from Scotland, and most significantly from Wales and Ireland. Not all immigrants were poor, but many were, especially in the wake of the Great Hunger of the 1840s, when destitute and starving Irish families arrived to congregate with their established compatriots, heaping poverty on top of poverty. The Irish quarters of the town were looked on with horror, providing a spectacle of filth and human misery and regarded as a threat to both health and social order. And while many poor – Irish or otherwise – raised themselves out of their condition by taking the opportunities provided by a growing national economy and the opening up of new continents, many – often the least enterprising – remained to struggle for survival in pitiful conditions.

This Liverpool, therefore, was rooted in poverty. Contemporaries debated cause and effect around the issues of overcrowding, disease, education, employment, and moral and spiritual condition. One thing, however, was clear: the situation could not be allowed to continue, and action was required. But by whom? And to what purpose? Beyond the coercive forces of the New Poor Law workhouse, government could do little. The community had to take responsibility, despite the disparity between the means and the need. The question increasingly became: how to direct resources most effectively to solve society's problems?

In the 18th and 19th centuries, the answer was found in charitable effort. England has a very long history of wealthy individuals and societies providing support for the disadvantaged. Before 1700, alms-giving and the construction of almshouses, hospitals and schools were, perhaps, the best-known types of charitable giving. Liverpool's relative insignificance in the Middle Ages meant that it did not inherit any of the great charitable institutions founded in many other towns at an early date.

Figure 5 *The Blue Coat School, School Lane (1716–18), paid for by Bryan Blundell, master mariner and future Mayor of Liverpool. It is the earliest standing building in the centre of the city. [AA047621]*

Figure 6 *Occupying the site of St George's Hall were, in the centre, the Infirmary (1749) and, flanking it on both sides, the Seamen's Hospital (1752), an almshouse for 'decayed seamen, their widows and children'. [Liverpool Record Office, Liverpool Libraries, Photographs and Small Prints]*

Instead, the first notable charitable efforts in the town date from the early and mid-18th century. The Blue Coat School was founded in 1708 and later moved to a new school building of 1716–18 (Fig 5), and the Infirmary and Seamen's Hospital opened in 1749 and 1752 respectively (Fig 6).

As the scale of need changed in the 19th century, so too did the charitable response and the response of the community. There were examples of the poor combining to help themselves. Much of this type of work may have gone unrecorded, leaving us with knowledge of only the most prominent cases like Kitty Wilkinson in the cholera years and the creation of the Mechanics' Institution. This has given us a top-down view of charity, a view recorded by the benefactors rather than the recipients. But the wealthy were not unresponsive to need. Great good work was done by many individuals and groups in alleviating distress through direct, sometimes spontaneous, giving of help to the needy. Critics, however, began to argue that, while doubtless motivated by generosity and a wish to do good, this approach – 'indiscriminate' charity – actually made the problem worse rather than better, since it could encourage attitudes of dependency and passivity. Men such as William Rathbone

11

advocated a sterner approach, which discouraged aid for the consequences of poverty – hunger, disease, poor housing and so on – and instead sought to lift the poor out of their condition by helping them to help themselves, particularly by demonstrating the benefits of a virtuous and upright life. A distinction was drawn between the 'deserving poor', those who through misfortune found themselves in difficulties, and the 'undeserving poor', whose depravity lay at the root of their condition. For the former, thrift, hard work and moral behaviour – exemplified, of course, in the lives of Liverpool's successful elite – were the path to the eradication of poverty. This cool-headed, detached policy was largely executed through domestic missions and the involvement of Liverpool's comfortable classes in visiting the needy, but it was also visible in the provision of educational facilities for the disadvantaged. This strand of charitable effort never entirely replaced the more direct methods of relieving the burden of poverty, but even together the two approaches were not able to eradicate the problem.

The needs of Liverpool's population were so diverse from the 18th to the 20th centuries that it is natural that charitable response was hugely varied. Powerful agencies became involved. It is not always easy to maintain a strict distinction between the contributions of private charitable effort and of the Corporation, for although the latter was limited in what it could do directly, it very often facilitated charitable work, particularly by grants of land for the construction of institutional buildings. Furthermore, during the 19th century, its powers grew to allow it to assume a much more direct role in addressing social problems. Religious bodies were also prominent in running or supporting charities. Much charitable enterprise was undertaken on a non-denominational basis, but there was undoubtedly sectarian competition – sometimes masked, sometimes overt – for the winning of lost souls, particularly between the Anglican and Roman Catholic churches. There were charities and societies for an immense range of disadvantaged or vulnerable groups – Jews, Scots, children, prostitutes, seamen, the blind, deaf and dumb, street urchins – and for particular purposes – shelter, education and health. Wherever Liverpool showed a need, it is likely that a charitable or collective response was developed.

Charity and Liverpool's wealthy elite

The motivation for charitable effort varied. The simple act of giving satisfied a human need and performed a Christian duty. It was not limited to the rich, for the response of the poor to the plight of their neighbours was an important, although largely unrecorded, aspect of charity. For the wealthy, it is now difficult to disentangle Christian kindness and an idealistic view of class relations from fear and self-interest, for it is possible to portray charitable effort both as genuinely altruistic and as calculated to stave off threats to a comfortable existence. Contemporaries saw other, more selfish, reasons for philanthropy; charity became a means of self-advancement, a sort of badge of citizenship. It was said of both Andrew Barclay Walker and William Brown that their large donations were calculated as steps on the road to a baronetcy.

Liverpool's wealthy elite, and a proportion of the comfortable classes below this level, were involved in charitable and institutional life through three main mechanisms. First, they created institutions which served the needs of their own society. While the city's dominant ethos remained commercial throughout the 18th and 19th centuries, there developed an awareness that a modern town was more than simply a place of exchange. It was also a focus for culture, learning and sociability, and money and energy were expended to put Liverpool into the mainstream of urban development. The clubs, assembly rooms, libraries and concert halls which were financed collectively through subscription or donations include many of the city's finest buildings, such as the Lyceum Club and Liverpool Library in Bold Street, the Wellington Rooms in Mount Pleasant and the political clubs on Dale Street (Figs 7, 8 and 9). The activities housed within these buildings helped to provide a sense of group identity to Liverpool's prosperous elite.

The second way in which the wealthy engaged with charitable effort was through their donations: they were the chief source of the funds which supported the huge number of charities operating in the city. Appeals were numerous, and they often contained a strong appeal to Christian duty. On the opening of the chapel at the Seamen's Orphanage

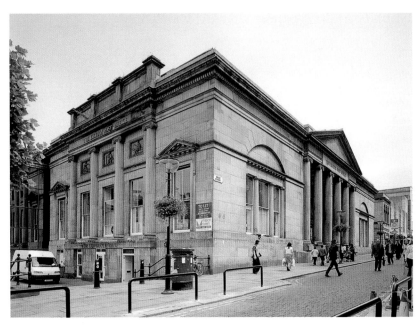

Figure 7 *The Lyceum, Bold Street (1800–2, Thomas Harrison), accommodated both the Lyceum Club and the Liverpool Library. [AA041059]*

Figure 8 (below, left) *Presenting a largely blank face externally, the Wellington Rooms (1814–16, Edmund Aikin) had a large ballroom, a card room and a supper room. [AA040896]*

Figure 9 (below) *The Conservative Club, Dale Street (1882–3, F and G Holme), is the largest of the political club buildings. [AA047775]*

in 1874, for example, the Archbishop of York called for donations and assured benefactors that 'you may be quite sure that you are doing the work of God and Christ, in feeding and sustaining the little ones whom He loves'.[3] Some of Liverpool's wealthiest families made substantial donations to charitable institutions. Andrew Barclay Walker is said to have contributed over £50,000 for the art gallery, and the roll call of benefactors to the university includes Walker again (who gave money for engineering laboratories), the sugar manufacturer Sir Henry Tate (who funded the library), and George Holt, the shipping line owner. The jam manufacturer W P Hartley followed William Rathbone's example of 'voluntary socialism', ultimately setting aside a third of his income for charitable purposes. It was, however, always a struggle to secure adequate funding, and the burden of supporting and co-ordinating charitable effort fell disproportionately on the older-established merchant and ship-owning dynasties, many of them Unitarians, like the Rathbones and Holts. Contemporary comment bemoaned the attitude of entrepreneurs who used Liverpool only as a 'happy hunting ground to make a fortune; then to carry it away to sunnier climes',[4] with the result that few wealthy families stayed for long to develop an interest in addressing the city's wider social problems. *The Times* proclaimed in 1874 that crime and health statistics allowed only one conclusion: 'Liverpool is a town whose leading inhabitants are negligent of their duties as citizens.'[5]

Some among the wealthy, perhaps those with both time and a social conscience, involved themselves more directly with charitable work or contributed in other ways to institutions. John Gladstone, father of William, financed the construction of Charitable Institutions House, in Slater Street, to assist charities by providing a base from which they could operate (Fig 10). Leading figures were heavily engaged in organisational tasks, none more so than William Rathbone, who helped to co-ordinate charitable effort through the District Provident Society and was personally responsible for establishing a new charity (the District Nursing Service) in 1859. Liverpool had nothing to match the philanthropic work of W H Lever across the Mersey at the model village of Port Sunlight, but one industrialist – W P Hartley – built a small village for his workers alongside his factory at Aintree in the 1880s (Fig 11).

Figure 10 *The small pedimented building is Charitable Institutions House, Slater Street, built c1825 to provide a base from which charities could operate. Its larger neighbour is St Andrew's Free School. [DP039561]*

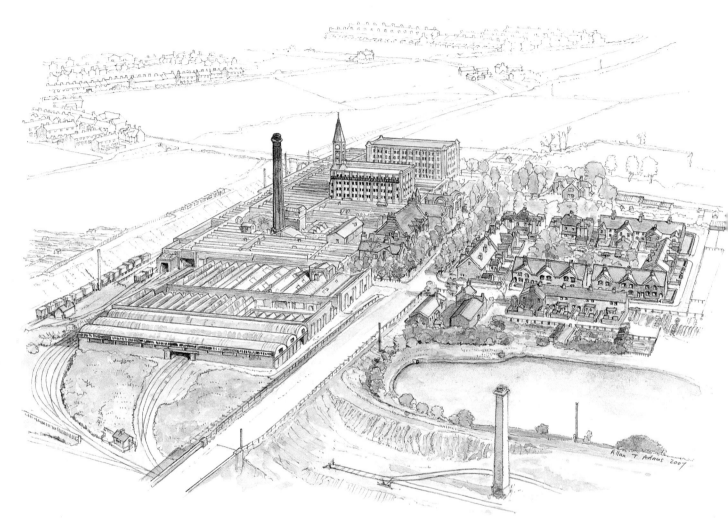

Figure 11 *Hartley Village, Aintree. W P Hartley's jam factory (1886, James F Doyle) dominated the landscape. It included a large dining hall for the workers. Next to the factory is a small village, made up of four rows of houses facing out from a square.*

Figure 12 *Memorial glass in the Anglican Cathedral: (top) Agnes Jones, the heroine of the Liverpool Workhouse infirmary and (bottom) Kitty Wilkinson, the poor Irish immigrant who established the first washhouse during the cholera epidemic of 1832. [DP039464, DP039465]*

Many comfortable families were involved in a range of activities designed to improve the condition of the needy. Women, especially, found in charitable work an outlet for their organisational abilities and an opportunity to engage with the great issues of the day. Agnes Jones, trained by Florence Nightingale, vastly improved conditions in the workhouse infirmary before succumbing to typhus in 1868 and Elizabeth Rathbone, from the great merchant dynasty, was instrumental in helping the poor Irish immigrant Kitty Wilkinson to set up public baths and washhouses in the 1830s (Fig 12). The plight of women forced into prostitution in the city became the focus of Josephine Butler's charitable efforts, and she founded the International Abolitionist Federation, which campaigned for state regulation of vice, holding its first congress in Liverpool in 1875. Many less prominent middle-class women became involved in visiting the poor to offer moral support. In one short-lived venture, it was proposed in 1898 to establish a 'settlement' where middle-class women could 'plant in a centre of vice, squalor and misery, a little oasis of education, refinement and sympathy',[6] and a house was taken in Everton Brow for the well-to-do volunteers to take up residence and provide an example to their poor neighbours.

Whatever the motives for charitable involvement, however partial the response by the comfortable classes to the scale of need, and despite the suspicion that charitable effort was no more than a palliative, the work of the Liverpool wealthy amounted to a considerable achievement. Countless thousands of people gained from charitable institutions: many lives (doubtless some souls too) were saved, and hope – however temporary – was offered to the desperate. Partial success was a measure of the immensity of the task.

Charitable work, with an emphasis on moral reform and through a judicious use of limited funds, shored up society sufficiently to prevent collapse. Without this effort, poverty, social instability, and a degraded environment would have taken an even greater toll.

CHAPTER 3

The poor and institutional life: Kirkdale and the wider urban scene

This interior view of Kirkdale Library in the early 20th century shows a packed house. [Liverpool Record Office, Liverpool Libraries, Photographs and Small Prints]

Even in prosperous times, Liverpool had large numbers of people living in poverty, and trade slumps pressed many more into a desperate struggle for survival until things picked up. Poverty bred squalor of all types: in 1848, the Borough Engineer wrote about the dreadful housing which 'engenders disease and conducts it to a fatal termination, encourages idleness and habits of filth too often accompanied by moral depravity, and wastes the hard-won earnings of the industrious poor'.[7] Graphic accounts of living conditions in insanitary courts and cellar dwellings were published, one in 1883 under the title of *Squalid Liverpool*, but getting the message out to the middle classes was hard work. A prolonged campaign by the magazine *The Porcupine* sounded a despairing note in 1863 when, despite its exposure of how the poor lived, 'the more comfortable parts of the public of Liverpool know nothing of such scenes ... . Probably not one in a hundred of them has ever been in one of those places, much less noted the regular gradations from the lowest depths to lower still.'[8]

The way in which Liverpool addressed the problems of the poor and needy is represented, at least partially, in the city's buildings, and this chapter will examine the infrastructure which was developed during the 19th century to provide support to the disadvantaged. To do this, it is necessary to broaden the scope to include both religious and governmental initiatives alongside the results of charitable effort. In the course of the century, the boundaries between different types of institutions became increasingly blurred, especially as government became engaged more heavily in addressing social problems. Church and chapel, government and private charitable effort all played a part. While not all aspects of institutional provision found expression in buildings, many important services were provided in structures which recall a different era in meeting society's needs.

The story of institutional buildings has, perhaps, two main aspects. The first is architectural and revolves around the creation of new building types for new needs and the adaptation of older ideas to the scale or nature of contemporary conditions. The change in the form and scale of hospitals and workhouses illustrates this aspect. The second concerns the way in which institutional buildings became deeply ingrained in the new urban landscapes of the 19th- and early 20th-century city. Some institutions were designed to serve the whole city or a considerable part of it, and were often, at least initially, centrally located; others were intended to serve local communities. Institutional buildings formed an integral part of the landscape of suburban Liverpool, and their impact will be explored through a focus on the township of Kirkdale, to the north of the city centre. Kirkdale was typical of those parts of Liverpool which fringed the river, but, like all dockside areas in the city, it has lost many of its institutional buildings: the township suffered heavily from wartime bombing, and huge swathes have been renewed in more recent decades. Evidence from other parts of the city will, therefore, be used, both where Kirkdale has lost its relevant structures and where other areas show important facets of institutional history never present there.

Kirkdale before 1850

Kirkdale lies on the north side of the city, between Liverpool and Bootle. In the early 19th century the land was still mainly in agricultural use, and the principal settlement, a small village with the chapel of St Mary, lay in the south-east corner of the township (Fig 13). Even at this early date, however, before Kirkdale began to be absorbed into greater Liverpool, institutions – some charitable, some governmental – figured prominently in the landscape.

Purely local needs were served by two small institutions shown on the mid-19th-century Ordnance Survey map: in the south of the township, close to the fast-advancing front line of Liverpool's expansion, was a small dispensary in Great Mersey Street which provided free advice, treatment and medicine to the poor; and close to St Mary's chapel there was a small Anglican church school, built in 1814 to provide elementary education for a few of the children of the township.

By the mid-19th century, Kirkdale had become something of a dumping ground for the problems of a wider area, and this had resulted in the construction of two large institutions. The need for a new prison had been satisfied in 1819, when the County House of Correction was

Figure 13 *Kirkdale in 1850: the agricultural landscape is already threatened by encroachment from the south and by the planting of the gaol and industrial homes. [Based on 1851 (surveyed 1845–9) Ordnance Survey 6" Lancashire Sheet 106]*

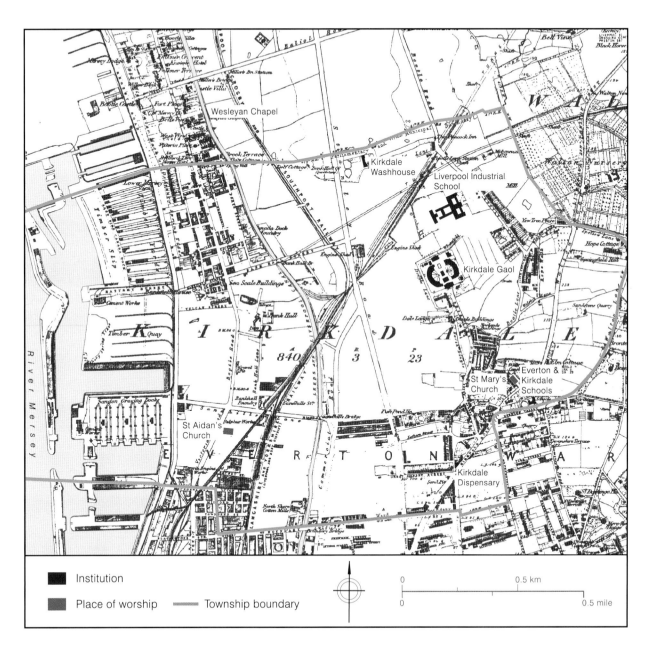

Wesleyan Chapel

Kirkdale Washhouse

Liverpool Industrial School

Kirkdale Gaol

St Mary's Church

Everton & Kirkdale Schools

St Aidan's Church

Kirkdale Dispensary

River Mersey

Institution

Place of worship

Township boundary

0   0.5 km

0   0.5 mile

Figure 14 *The County House of Correction, built in 1819 with two large crescent-shaped cell blocks, was also known as Kirkdale Gaol. [Liverpool Record Office, Liverpool Libraries, Photographs and Small Prints]*

built in the northern part of the township. A Sessions House was also built nearby to house the courts which dispatched criminals to the Gaol. The Gaol and Sessions House were imposing buildings, large in scale and of impressive architectural quality (Figs 14 and 15), and at first they stood in glorious isolation surrounded by fields. Both have been demolished, but Sessions Road is a reminder of their former presence.

Liverpool chose Kirkdale, newly taken within the borough, as the place to which it could remove one of its greatest social problems, that of pauperism, specifically 'juvenile pauperism'. This reached a crisis point in the 1840s, and it was decided to construct 'Industrial Schools' to house and educate destitute children. The outermost part of Kirkdale was selected as a remote outpost of the workhouse on Brownlow Hill. The Liverpool Industrial Schools opened in 1845, and the vast building – designed to accommodate over 1,100 children – indicated the scale of the problem facing the growing city (Fig 16). The boys were taught trades – there was even a ship in the grounds to assist in demonstrating the arts of seamanship – and the girls were prepared for work as domestic servants. The severe Tudor style of the schools, their size and their proximity to the prison must have given this part of Kirkdale a grim character in the mid-19th century.

Figure 15 *The County Sessions House at Kirkdale: convicted criminals could start their sentence immediately in the adjacent gaol. [Liverpool Record Office, Liverpool Libraries, Photographs and Small Prints]*

Figure 16 *The Liverpool Industrial Schools, opened in 1845 as a shelter and school for juvenile paupers. [Liverpool Record Office, Liverpool Libraries,* from West Derby Union: An Outline of the Main Features of the West Derby Union. *(Liverpool: 1925)]*

Kirkdale and Liverpool in the second half of the 19th century

From the 1840s, Liverpool's tentacles began to stretch out to explore Kirkdale's open spaces. The township has a frontage to the Mersey, and by 1860 this was entirely lined with docks. Behind the docks there developed a huge railway infrastructure, with goods yards and goods stations interspersed with timber yards and streets of warehouses. Inland again, east of Commercial Road, a dense network of streets of terraced houses,

Table 1: Institutional buildings in Kirkdale and environs, *c*1900

Type	Denomination	Kirkdale	Environs	Total
Churches and chapels	Anglican	4	6	10
	Nonconformist	13	9	22
	Roman Catholic	3	4	7
	Other	2		2
Convent	Roman Catholic		1	1
Mission Halls	Anglican	2	2	4
	Nonconformist	2	1	3
	'Unsectarian'	2	1	3
	Other	1		1
Schools	Anglican	4	5	9
	Nonconformist	4	4	8
	Roman Catholic	3	1	4
	Other	7	5	12
Industrial schools/institutes		6	4	10
Education (libraries etc)		1	2	3
Health (hospitals, bathhouses)		2	2	4
Police/Gaol		3	1	4
Meeting Rooms, Halls		4	2	6
Clubs		2		2
Sailors' Home		1		1
Orphanage	Roman Catholic		1	1
Roman Catholic College			1	1
Christian Police Institute			1	1
Totals		66	53	119

Sources: Ordnance Survey 1890 1:500 plans; Ordnance Survey 1906–7 1:2500, sheets 106.2, 106.6

complete by 1900, climbed up the hill towards Everton, Anfield and Walton, and Kirkdale became part of the mass of built-up Liverpool: only the name of Boundary Street shows where one ended and the other began. The newly built houses were small but by no means inadequate. Built by speculators, they largely post-dated the by-laws which stipulated minimum standards of construction and density. This was, therefore, by 1900 an improved urban environment, with solidly built houses, water supplies and sewers. Kirkdale was certainly not classic Liverpool slum territory: that lay immediately to the south, in the Vauxhall Road and Scotland Road areas, where the notorious courts and cellar dwellings remained from an earlier era. But this does not mean that Kirkdale was immune to social problems: it soon came to have its share of poverty and deprivation.

This evolving suburban landscape was the theatre where many of the contemporary solutions to the plight of the poor were implemented. The institutional map of Kirkdale, like its landscape, was utterly transformed by 1900. The newly formed communities were supported by a wide range of institutions, some of them governmental, illustrating the expansion in the role of the state in providing services; others religious, showing how the different denominations competed for souls; and others charitable (*see* Table 1 and Fig 17, over).

Law and religion

Authority was represented in Kirkdale by the long arm of the law. As Liverpool grew, so did its lawlessness, and efforts were made to provide a police presence in the main trouble spots. One of four new branch police stations for the Liverpool constabulary was built in Athol Street, just beyond the township's southern boundary, in 1852. Set behind a high perimeter wall, this 'bridewell' was like a fortress in the unruly dockland area (Fig 18). A second dockland police station was built on Derby Road. As Kirkdale came to be built up with improved housing, the police presence adopted a friendlier face, represented in Kirkdale by the combined Police and Fire Station on Westminster Road, built in 1885 to designs by the Liverpool Borough Surveyor, Thomas

Figure 18 *Athol Street Bridewell, built in 1852: the high perimeter walls provided some defence in this volatile area. [Liverpool Record Office, Liverpool Libraries, Photographs and Small Prints]*

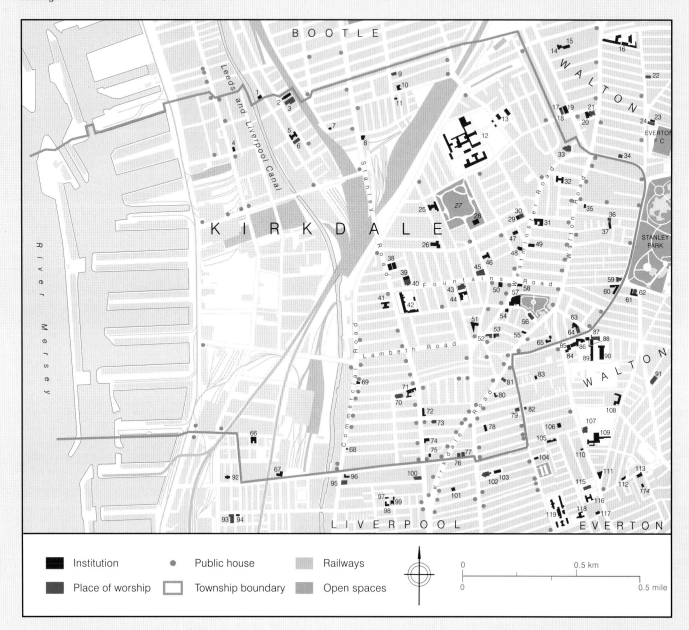

Figure 17 *Kirkdale* c1900: *the township itself had 66 institutions, including churches, chapels, schools, police stations and charitable buildings.*

Institution

Place of worship

Public house

Township boundary

Railways

Open spaces

0   0.5 km

0   0.5 mile

Key

1 Baptist Chapel, Brasenose Road
2 St Alexander's RC School, St John's Road
3 St Alexander's RC Church, St John's Road 1867/1884
4 Bridewell, Derby Road
5 St Paul's School, St John's Road 1868
6 St Paul's Church, St John's Road 1868
7 Mission Hall, Oriel Road
8 Bankhall Girls Institute, Stanley Road 1889
9 Wesleyan Methodist Chapel, Miranda Road
10 Congregational Mission Hall, Marsh Street
11 Mission Room (unsectarian), Miranda Road
12 Liverpool Industrial Schools/Kirkdale Homes, Rumney Road
13 School, Westminster Road
14 St Francis de Sales RC School, Hale Road
15 St Francis de Sales RC Chapel, Hale Road
16 Arnot Street Schools, Arnot Street 1884
17 Baptist Sunday School, Roxburgh Street
18 Baptist Church, Roxburgh Street
19 Technical Institute, Carisbrooke Street
20 Methodist Sunday School, Harlech Street
21 Wesleyan Methodist Chapel, Harlech Street
22 Chapel, Goodison Road
23 Parish Room, Gladwys Street
24 St Luke's Church, Goodison Road
25 School, Fonthill Road
26 School, Orwell Road
27 *Kirkdale Gaol, Orwell Road*
28 Free Library, Brook Street
29 Congregational Sunday School, Orwell Road
30 Congregational Chapel, Orwell Road 1872
31 Police and Fire Station, Westminster Road 1885
32 St Lawrence's School, Croyland Street 1873
33 St Lawrence's Church, Barlow Lane 1881
34 Presbyterian Church, Spellow Lane 1891
35 Welsh Presbyterian Chapel (1906 Hall), Salop Street
36 Free Gospel Chapel, Tetlow Street 1860/1877
37 Sunday School, Tetlow Street
38 Gordon Working Lads Institute, Stanley Road 1886
39 Presbyterian Sunday School, Wykeham Street
40 Presbyterian Church, Fountains Road 1876–81
41 School, Daisy Street
42 Stanley Hospital, Stanley Road 1867/1874
43 Church, Fountains Road
44 School, Fonthill Road
45 St John's RC Church, Fountains Road 1885
46 School, Sessions Road
47 Nonconformist Meeting Room, Churnet Street
48 Hall, Westminster Road
49 Skelmersdale Masonic Hall, Westminster Road
50 Synagogue, Fountains Road
51 YMCA Club, Foley Street
52 Baptist Tabernacle, Westminster Road 1892
53 *Baptist Chapel and School, Bousfield Street*
54 School, Archer Street
55 Girls' Home Industrial School, Kirkdale Road
56 St Mary's Church, Kirkdale Road 1835
57 Public Baths, Westminster Road 1876
58 Conservative Club, Westminster Road
59 Baptist Chapel, Walton Lane 1875
60 School, Walton Lane
61 Sunday School, Anfield Road
62 Welsh Calvinist Chapel, Anfield Road
63 Presbyterian Church School, Royal Street
64 Presbyterian Church, Everton Valley
65 St Mary's School, Everton Valley
66 Sailors' Home, Luton Street
67 St Alban's RC School, Boundary Street
68 St Aidan's Mission Hall, Commercial Road
69 Congregational Mission House, Commercial Road
70 St Aidan's Church, Latham Street 1875
71 St Aidan's School, Latham Street
72 St Alphonsus' School, Stanley Road
73 Welsh Independent Chapel, Great Mersey Street
74 Kirkdale Industrial Ragged School, Stanley Road
75 Mission House, C of E, Back Boundary Street
76 Welsh Wesleyan Methodist Chapel, Boundary Street
77 Primitive Methodist Chapel, Boundary Street
78 Hall, Crete Street/Mitylene Street
79 Welsh Calvinist Methodist Chapel, Netherfield Road
80 Mission Hall (unsectarian), Kirk Street
81 St Alphonsus' RC Church, Kirkdale Road
82 Free United Methodist Chapel, Netherfield Road
83 St Chad's Mission Room, Devonshire Place
84 Congregational Sunday School, St Domingo Road
85 Congregational Church, Everton Valley
86 Convent of the Sisters of Notre Dame, Everton Valley
87 St Chad's Church, Everton Valley
88 St Chad's Sunday School, Everton Valley
89 Collegiate School, Everton Valley
90 Major Lester School, Everton Valley
91 St Cuthbert's Church, Robson Street
92 Baths, Beacon Street
93 St Alban's RC Church, Athol Street 1849
94 The Albany Reading Room, Athol Street
95 Wesleyan Methodist Chapel, Commercial Road
96 Wesleyan Methodist School, Commercial Road
97 Presbyterian Mission Room, Hankin Street
98 St James the Less School, Athol Street
99 Police Station, Athol Street 1852
100 St James the Less Church, Stanley Road
101 School, Dalrymple Street
102 Christ Church, Gt Homer Street
103 Christ Church School, Anderson Street
104 Hall, Netherfield Road
105 School, York Terrace
106 Northern Institute, York Terrace
107 Our Lady Immaculate RC Church, St Domingo Road
108 RC Orphanage for Boys, Beacon Lane
109 St Edward's RC College, St Domingo Road
110 Mission Room (unsectarian), St Domingo Road
111 Everton Library, St Domingo Road 1896
112 St George's Infant School/Hall, Mere Lane
113 School, Mere Lane
114 *Manual Training School, Lansdowne Place*
115 St George's Church, St Domingo Road
116 St George's School, St Domingo Road
117 Christian Police Institute, Mission Place
118 Liverpool Industrial School (Girls), Northumberland Terrace
119 City Hospital North, Netherfield Road

[Reproduced from the 1890 Ordnance Survey 10ft: 1 mile town plans; and 1906 revision Ordnance Survey 25": 1 mile plans, Lancashire 106.2, 6. The entries in italics only appear on the 1890 version.]

Figure 19 *Westminster Road Police and Fire Station, Kirkdale (1885, Thomas Shelmerdine). The complex included a large parade room at the rear.* [DP039439, DP039429]

Shelmerdine (Fig 19). The lively architectural style and direct connection with the street contrast with the earlier generation of grim bridewells, perhaps an indication of either more orderly conditions in the 1880s or a desire to present a different, less repressive, image within the community which it served.

The role of the churches – Established, Nonconformist and Roman Catholic, as well as minor sects – in missionary work in Liverpool's suburbs was of huge importance, and places of worship form one of the dominating elements within the developing suburban landscape: by 1906, there were 22 in Kirkdale township.[9] Some, like the Baptist Chapel on Walton Lane, occupied prominent main road sites (Fig 20), but most –

Figure 20 *The Baptist Chapel, Walton Lane, built in 1875, forms a prominent landmark opposite Stanley Park.* [DP039474]

Figure 21 *Presbyterian Church, Spellow Lane, built in 1891, interrupts a terrace of housing. [DP039431]*

Figure 22 *The former Salvation Army Barracks in Antonio Street, Bootle, squeezed into a plot at a bend in the road. [DP039437]*

including the Anglican churches – were on lesser roads. Some of the chapels and one of the Roman Catholic churches – St Alphonsus – bit deeply into the residential landscape, squeezed into what were little more than house plots within a terrace (Fig 21). The same applies to some of the Mission Halls built by different denominations, small buildings set right in the heart of the community. They brought spiritual comfort to the poor, and often contained reading rooms and classrooms (Fig 22). Not all were denominational, for two of the Kirkdale mission halls were

Figure 23 *The Liverpool Domestic Mission, Mill Street, Toxteth, was run by Unitarians on a non-sectarian basis. [Liverpool Record Office, Liverpool Libraries, from Hope 1903]*

shown on Ordnance Survey maps as 'unsectarian'. The Liverpool Domestic Mission, in Mill Street, on the south side of the city (and therefore not in Kirkdale), had a chapel, classrooms, a meeting hall for up to 600, and a reading room (Fig 23). In 1903, it was written that 'although its missionaries and most of its workers are Unitarians, the Mission has no proselytizing or sectarian aim; it simply seeks, by personal intercourse with the poor, to help them spiritually and socially, without distinction of sect or creed or party'.[10]

Education

The hectic pace of Liverpool's expansion in the mid- and late 19th century meant that its growing population had to endure a period of acute instability, during which the provision of services lagged behind the needs of new communities. The lack of adequate education for the poor was one of the most serious deficiencies and was increasingly seen as a cause of poverty, vice and irreligion. Instruction in morals, discipline and useful skills came to be a central part of charitable effort in the city and the focus of efforts to turn Liverpool's vulnerable children into productive, upright citizens.

A number of parallel initiatives attempted to provide education for poor children. The Blue Coat School (*see* Fig 5) had offered instruction for a few since the early 18th century, but Liverpool's growth had made it inadequate a century later. Other schools, funded by charitable donations, developed to meet the needs of different parts of the community: a Welsh Charity School was built in Russell Street in 1804, and Irish children were catered for in the Hibernian School, Pleasant Street, founded in 1807 (Fig 24). The churches led the way in the

Figure 24 *The Hibernian School, Pleasant Street, was founded in 1807 to educate poor Irish children.* [AA047707]

Figure 25 *The Congregational Sunday School on Orwell Road, stands out because of its use of yellow brick, an unusual material in Liverpool. [DP039427]*

suburbs, taking up plots for schools as well as for places of worship. Kirkdale illustrates the process by which elementary education was introduced in the expanding suburbs. The Anglican school of St Mary's, in Everton Valley, was the first to be built in Kirkdale, before 1850, and as housing progressively covered the fields the different denominations responded by building elementary schools, some next to, others near to, the governing church or chapel (Figs 25, 26 and 27). In the far north of the township, St John's Road had a neat balance, with the Roman Catholic St Alexander's Church (1867) and school on one side and, close by on the other side, the Anglican St Paul's Church and school (1868). Around Everton Valley, the denominations jostled for space, with St Chad's Church and school (Anglican), the Roman Catholic Convent of the Sisters of Notre Dame and its collegiate school, the Congregational

Figure 26 *The Roman Catholic school of St John, North Dingle, Kirkdale, built in the early 20th century next to the earlier presbytery and church. The school had a roof-top playground. [DP039423]*

Figure 27 *St Lawrence's Church of England School, Croyland Street, Kirkdale, built in 1873, stands away from its mother church, formerly on Barlow Lane, a little distance away. [DP039339]*

Church and school, and the Anglican St Mary's School, not to mention the Girls' Home Industrial School run by Canon Lester (Fig 28).

More advanced education was also available to a limited number of poor children. The Mechanics' Institution, founded in 1825, was originally intended principally for the instruction of adults, but in its new premises, built between 1835 and 1837, it quickly established higher and lower schools for boys, the division being based not on age but on the nature of the education provided. A girls' school was founded in Blackburne House, Hope Street, in 1844. This non-sectarian education had denominational counterparts in the Collegiate Institution, built on Shaw Street in 1840–3, which offered an Anglican education, and the Roman Catholic St Francis Xavier College, which opened in new

Figure 28 *The Convent of the Sisters of Notre Dame, Everton Valley, is the dominant building in this group, but a school, a training college and a chapel give an institutional character to this side of the street.* [DP039596]

premises in Salisbury Street in 1855–6. The Collegiate Institution had upper, middle and lower schools, the last providing an education for children destined for clerical work in offices (Fig 29). The schools were kept more or less strictly segregated within the institution: even the playground was divided into separate areas.

The efforts of the denominations in establishing elementary schools always lagged behind educational need during the middle decades of the 19th century. The city was expanding rapidly, new communities were forming, and school places were limited. Liverpool's streets teemed with uneducated children, many destitute and lacking socially useful skills. In the mid-19th century Father James Nugent, the Roman Catholic priest, estimated that there were about 23,000 children running wild around the Liverpool docks. The number seems scarcely credible, but clearly there was a problem to be addressed, one which included shelter (for many of the children were homeless), morals and education.

Figure 29 *The Collegiate Institution, Shaw Street, opened in 1843. The architect was Harvey Lonsdale Elmes, and the building contained upper, middle and lower schools providing different types of education.* [DP039410]

Figure 30 *Training ships on the Mersey off Birkenhead: the* Conway *(an officers' training ship), the* Indefatigable *(a naval cadets' ship), and the* Akbar *(the reformatory ship for Protestant boys).* [*Liverpool Record Office, Liverpool Libraries, Photographs and Small Prints*]

These were provided for some of Liverpool's street children in reformatory or industrial schools, administering something of the 'short, sharp shock' treatment exemplified in the Liverpool Industrial Schools (*see* Fig 16). Perhaps the harshest environment was encountered in the reformatory training ships which wallowed in the Mersey off Birkenhead (Fig 30). These wooden warship hulks, sad shadows of their fighting past, were intended as a means of turning convicted juvenile criminals into useful citizens and of keeping them, at least temporarily, out of prison. The regime on board instilled morals and trained the boys in seamanship. Two of the ships – the *Akbar* (Protestant, opened for business in 1855) and the *Clarence* (Roman Catholic, 1864) – were more or less strictly denominational in intake. They cannot have been popular: in 1884 the Catholic boys set fire to their ship, and in 1887 the Protestant boys mutinied.

On land, 'Industrial' or 'Ragged' schools were established as a response to the crisis in child care. Similar to the workhouse industrial school at Kirkdale, but not funded by the parish rate, they were established to shelter, feed and educate the poorest children. A national Ragged School Union was formed in 1844, and by 1853 32 schools had been established in Liverpool. The churches were the driving force behind the movement, inspired in part by a spirit of competition. The Roman Catholic Sisters of Charity ran St Francis Xavier's Ragged School and Soup Kitchen and provided nourishment for mind, body and soul. As well as the school and the chapel, there were good meals for the hungry: 'one day the fare included bacon and greens, but the staple diet is lob-scouse, or stewed potatoes and meat, or strong pea soup'. It was said in 1867 that 'Angels may rejoice to see the poor boys ... educated, Christianized and fed from the donations of the poor'.[11]

The efforts of Roman Catholic churchmen such as Monsignor Nugent in setting up and running ragged schools were matched by those of Canon Major Lester, the Anglican vicar of St Mary's, Kirkdale. He opened a mission room in Kirkdale Road in 1856, a second one in Christopher Street in 1862, and a third, in what became Major Street, in the same year (Fig 31). The Major Street Ragged School had a kitchen (used as a soup kitchen in winter), schoolrooms on two floors, and workshops for teaching trades – tailoring, printing, matchbox making, paper-bag making. These institutions must have offered a lifeline, both to the poorest children and to their families, unable to support them or offer them any prospects. Something of their achievement is captured in a sentimental ballad published in 1906:

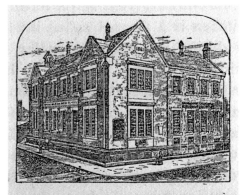

THE MAJOR STREET RAGGED SCHOOLS

Figure 31 *The Major Street Ragged School, Kirkdale, one of the industrial schools founded by Canon Major Lester to provide shelter, sustenance, education and moral training for the vagrant children of the township. [Liverpool Record Office, Liverpool Libraries, from Rev A H Grey-Edwards 1906,* A Great Heart or the Life of Canon Major Lester MA *(London)]*

I have no home, none to protect!
Oh! Save me or I'll die;
In the cold grave my parents sleep
And I'm a homeless boy.

After being taken in to the ragged school, this model of the deserving poor could claim:

My humble thanks I now return;
My soul is filled with joy;
I'm at the Kirkdale Ragged School,
But not a homeless boy.[12]

None of the ragged schools survives today, but the work of Canon Major Lester and Monsignor Nugent is still remembered in the city.

The 1870 Education Act marked a turning point in the provision of education for the poor, for it introduced direct government action into the picture. Ultimately, of course, the state was to be the dominant supplier of education, but the 1870 Act simply empowered local authorities to fill the gaps left by the denominations and charity in the provision of elementary education. The Liverpool School Board responded vigorously: by 1902 it had built 42 schools across the borough, at least four of them in Kirkdale. While the denominational schools, especially the Sunday schools, were often small adjuncts to the church or chapel, the board schools stood alone and were among the most prominent buildings in the landscape, representing both the power of the public purse in answering social need and a new philosophy about the role of government in the lives of ordinary people. The layout of the schools follows a common pattern. The larger buildings were of two main storeys, with well-lit classrooms grouped around a central hall. There were usually separate entrances for boys and girls, and bells, sometimes housed in turrets or towers, imposed time discipline. The exterior designs varied in elaboration. Perhaps the most ornate were the Arnot Street Schools by Edmund Kirby, built in 1884, Tudor Perpendicular in style and built in bright red brick. The street elevation is busy, with hipped dormers, an oriel window, and a central block rising above the rest to end in a bell turret (Fig 32). Such buildings must have made as powerful an impression on the newly constructed landscape as they did on the lives of the children who passed through their gates.

Figure 32 *The Arnot Street Schools, Walton, just beyond the Kirkdale township boundary, are one of the finest of Liverpool's board schools, built in 1884 to designs by Edmund Kirby. [DP039335]*

Education: institutes for young people

Despite the existence by the 1880s of a large number of schools providing elementary education, there was a need for a complementary type of institution, one which encouraged the productive use of free time for boys, girls and youths. Both the north and south ends of Liverpool were affected by rowdyism and indolence, often associated with drinking in public houses. In these parts of Liverpool, one could never be more than a few yards away from a drinking hole, and easy access to alcohol, together with the example of disreputable youths who frequented the pubs, were temptations to the impressionable. Strenuous efforts, therefore, were made to provide facilities which would offer an alternative use of leisure time or slack time between jobs. In the south end of Liverpool, the Florence Institute was built in 1889 by the merchant Bernard Hall to provide (for boys only – local girls had nothing to match the Florence) 'religious and moral instruction of a Christian undenominational character, to be given by means of classes for the study of the Bible and Christian teaching and by unsectarian religious services'.[13] In the north end, Kirkdale had both the Gordon Working Lads Institute – built in 1886 by a merchant and shipowner, William Cliff, in memory of his son (an example of private sorrow inspiring public charity) – and the Bankhall Girls Institute, funded by Thomas Worthington Cookson, another merchant and shipowner, opened in 1889.

These institutes made efforts to extend what they offered beyond Bible classes, which on their own might not have drawn large numbers of youths away from the smoke room of the pubs. The problem of unskilled labour, always prone to unemployment, was addressed through technical and practical training. The Gordon Working Lads Institute had metalworking and woodworking shops, offered training in plumbing, and held drawing, arithmetic and writing classes. The Florence Institute had a similar range of facilities. Most important in character forming, however, was the emphasis on discipline, instilled in music (both the Gordon Working Lads and the Florence had brass bands), sports and drill training. At the Working Lads Institute, there was 'a stand containing 200

Snider carbines, presented to the Cliff Brigade by Mr William Cliff, the Honorary Colonel'. Drill instruction, it was felt, 'develops the qualities of soldiery steadiness and self-respect'.[14]

All three institutes made an impact on their neighbourhood and on their communities (Figs 33, 34 and 35). They were deliberately sited on main roads, on corner sites, and they are large enough to dominate their vicinity, overshadowing the public houses which they were designed to rival. They introduce a modest amount of architectural variety to the

Figure 33 *Bankhall Girls Institute, Stanley Road, Kirkdale, built in 1889 in Jacobean style: the large first-floor windows light a main meeting room. [AA047772]*

Figure 34 *Gordon Working Lads Institute, Stanley Road, Kirkdale, designed by David Walker and opened in 1886, occupies a whole block between side streets off the main road. Behind the 1886 building is a large drill hall, added to the complex in the 1930s and used now as a gymnasium. [AA047773]*

Figure 35 *The Florence Institute, Mill Street, Toxteth, opened in 1889. This is the largest and most decorative of this group of institutes, and the turret, originally capped by an onion dome, acted as an eye catcher. [DP039362]*

street scene. Bankhall is in a Jacobean style, in red brick with stone dressings, mullioned and transomed windows and a roof line with shaped gables, arcaded balustrade and finials. The Working Lads Institute is larger, occupying a whole block. The tall first-floor windows and stepped gables give it much greater height than might be expected in a two-and-a-half storey building, and the eclectic Flemish style, carried out mainly in brick, catches the attention in an otherwise largely utilitarian street. The largest of the three is the Florence Institute, built in bright orange brick and terracotta, but this time in Tudor Gothic style with canted bay windows and shaped gables. The dominating feature here is a corner tower, once capped by an onion dome, probably a deliberate attempt to draw the eye away from the local public houses: there was one directly opposite the Florence, and another on one corner of its block.

A contemporary account of the Working Lads building, perhaps a piece of propaganda representing aspirations rather than reality, remarked on how it 'nightly sheds a flood of light upon its surroundings'.[15] The interiors of the institutes, while mainly utilitarian, were also capable of making an impression. The same account emphasises the brightly lit rooms and the quality of the fittings, perhaps an attempt to give to poor lads a glimpse of refinement. Undoubtedly the most impressive element of the institutes were their meeting halls, set on the first floor. At the Working Lads, the hall could accommodate 600 (Fig 36), but the Florence topped that with space for 1,000. Public entertainments were held in the halls, embedding the institutes in the life of the community.

Figure 37 *The Mechanics' Institution, Mount Street (1835–7, A H Holme). The Classical style links the architecture to the secular character of the institute. The building now forms part of the Liverpool Institute for Performing Arts (LIPA). [AA040506]*

Education: institutes for adults, libraries

The desire to educate adults and thereby to give them the means to escape poverty found expression in a range of institutions, not all of them represented in Kirkdale. The most prominent was the Mechanics' Institution, founded in 1825 with gifts from, among others, John Gladstone, William's father. Mechanics' institutions were built, usually with donations from leading local figures, in many growing towns in this period, and all aimed to provide useful instruction, of a secular kind, for working men so that they might be able to better their condition. They represent perhaps the most powerful example of the poor combining to raise themselves out of their condition through education. In Liverpool, an extensive new building was constructed in Mount Street, near the centre of the city, in 1835–7, and its size and architectural splendour, at least externally, rivalled the cultural institutions of the wealthy. Built in smooth sandstone in a Grecian Classical style, it has a heavy central portico with Ionic columns (Fig 37). The design lent dignity to the

Figure 38 *The Walton Institute, Sefton Street, Walton, was built in 1874 at the end of a terrace of houses. [DP039492]*

purpose of the institution, which was, Lord Brougham announced when the foundation stone was laid, 'to diffuse the blessings of knowledge amongst all classes of the community; to afford the means of instruction in the most useful arts to by far the most useful members of this great community (cheers) ... from which may be expected to spring ... the happiest results upon the conditions and morals of the people (cheers)'.[16] Internally, there were reading rooms, classrooms and laboratories grouped around a large lecture hall, where public lectures and readings, including one in 1844 by Charles Dickens, were held. Less formal access to learning was provided by the William Brown Library, which opened in 1860 and proved very popular with working people.

Later in the 19th century, similar objectives lay behind the provision of much smaller, local institutions, again funded by donations from the wealthy. Reading rooms were planted in some areas to make learning more accessible to the poorer levels of society: there was one – the Albany Reading Room, a real missionary effort – in Athol Street, close to the docks just beyond Kirkdale's southern boundary, in 1900. Local institutes could provide a venue for education and public meetings. Some were simple buildings: the Walton Institute was built in 1874 at the end of a terrace of houses (Fig 38). More outstanding architecturally are two further examples. The Aintree Institute, given by W P Hartley for his workers in 1896, is in a collegiate Perpendicular Gothic and towers massively over its surroundings (Fig 39). The Gregson Memorial Institute and Museum, in Garmoyle Road, Wavertree, opened in 1895, is much smaller but stands out in its suburban setting by its polychrome brickwork: inside, it has a large meeting hall decorated with art nouveau tiles (Figs 40 and 41).

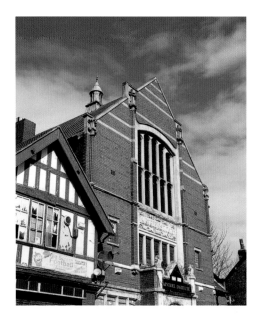

Figure 39 *The Aintree Institute, built in 1896 by W P Hartley for the people of Aintree, soars above the roofline of surrounding buildings. [DP039479]*

Figure 40 *The Gregson Memorial Institute and Museum, Garmoyle Road, Wavertree: typical Liverpool polychrome brickwork is used in this modest domestic-scale design. [DP006355]*

Figure 41 *Inside, the Gregson Memorial Institute and Museum has a large lecture hall and is decorated with art nouveau tiles and fittings. [DP006344, DP006337]*

Figure 42 (right) *A thirst for knowledge: children in Kensington Library, early 20th century. [Liverpool Record Office, Liverpool Libraries, Photographs and Small Prints]*

Figure 43 (left) *Everton Library, St Domingo Road (1896, Thomas Shelmerdine), perhaps the finest of the Liverpool branch libraries: the façade is enlivened by carved low-relief stone panels. [DP039344]*

In the late 19th century, the first free branch libraries were built in Liverpool through a combination of Corporation investment and substantial philanthropic donations. The first to be built, in 1890, was in Kensington (Fig 42), and this, like later branch libraries of this period, was designed by the Corporation surveyor Thomas Shelmerdine. Everton Library followed in 1896 and is, perhaps, the most ornamental of the group (Fig 43), the richness of the architecture proclaiming the building as a beacon of learning. Others, however, were almost equally impressive, standing out in their suburban settings as places where learning could be brought to the people in elegant surroundings. Although

Figure 44 *Toxteth Branch Library, Windsor Street (1900–2, Thomas Shelmerdine): this was opened with great ceremony by Andrew Carnegie, who promised to help with the construction of further branches in the city: exterior (above); copper memorial plaque recording the opening by Carnegie (left). [DP039566, DP039603]*

relatively small in scale, the branch libraries are among the most distinguished public buildings of the period in the city. The leading benefactor in their construction was Andrew Carnegie, who opened Toxteth Library in 1902 (Fig 44) and offered £13,000 towards the building of a second library, built in West Derby. Kirkdale had a branch library by 1906, built on part of the site formerly occupied by the gaol (Fig 45). It received a direct hit by incendiary bombs in 1941. A second library, on Stanley Road, was built in the 1920s, and this survives, although with a different use.

Figure 45 *Kirkdale's first branch library, in Brook Street, built in the first years of the 20th century: the building was destroyed in the blitz of 1941. [Liverpool Record Office, Liverpool Libraries, Photographs and Small Prints]*

Health

If education, in all its different forms, dominated charitable effort – or at least its built expression – in the 19th century, a concern to provide better health services came a close second. All social classes were threatened by disease and were subject to both accident and the normal hazards of contemporary life, such as child bearing. Not all, however, could afford medical care, and the plight of the poor began to cause concern in the mid-18th century. The result of this concern was the opening in 1749 of the Liverpool Infirmary, on the site of St George's Hall, one of the first hospitals in the country to be built through local, charitable donations (*see* Fig 6). Demand eventually made it inadequate, and a larger hospital was built in 1821–4 on Brownlow Street. While this sufficed for a few years, Liverpool's very rapid expansion soon created the need for more hospitals, located closer to the new centres of population: Northern and Southern

Figure 46 *Stanley Hospital, Stanley Road, Kirkdale, as rebuilt in 1874: only the gate piers now remain. [Liverpool Record Office, Liverpool Libraries, Photographs and Small Prints]*

Hospitals were built close to the docks in 1834 and 1842. Later further general hospitals were built around the city. The people of Kirkdale had access to a local hospital – the Stanley Hospital – by 1867, and this was rebuilt on a larger scale in 1874 (Fig 46). They were also served by a new, larger central Royal Infirmary in Pembroke Place (1887–90, to designs by Alfred Waterhouse). In addition, a large number of specialist hospitals, all founded with charitable donations, together with workhouse infirmaries, were constructed in the 19th century, giving Liverpool a highly complex system of caring for the sick and afflicted. Something of the variety in hospital provision will be explored in Chapter 4.

Health depended partly on cleanliness, in the home and more widely, and Liverpool was one of the cities which pioneered the provision of public baths and washhouses. The Corporation built public baths in George's Dock in 1828, but this was more a leisure facility than an answer to the town's public health needs. During 1832, cholera struck Liverpool and a connection was made between the incidence of the disease and the squalor in which many poor people lived. Kitty Wilkinson, a poor Irish immigrant living in Vauxhall ward, set up the cellar of her house as a washhouse for the use of neighbours, principally to allow them to wash clothes and bedding which had come into contact with cholera victims.

What started as a local solution prompted by Christian fellow feeling soon grew into a more concerted response. Aided by the support of Mrs Elizabeth Rathbone, a campaign for public facilities developed, and the Corporation responded by constructing a public baths and washhouse – the first in the country – in Upper Frederick Street, on the south side of the city, in 1842 (Fig 47). Kitty Wilkinson was installed as supervisor, and the building had individual bathrooms, a washhouse with 21 tubs and a drying stove. The room for washing infected clothes could be used without charge on presentation of a note from a medical officer. Other baths and washhouses followed: the plans of the buildings show areas for bathing and other areas for washing and drying clothes: significantly, parts of the buildings were segregated for the treatment of 'infected clothes' (Fig 48). Liverpool prided itself on its construction of showcase baths and washhouses, but the Corporation's policy was criticised at the

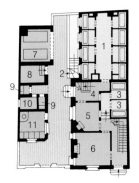

1 Bathrooms
2 Stair to washhouse
3 Private bathroom
4 Stair to bath and
   reading rooms
5 Waiting room
6 Parlour
7 Boiler house
8 Coals
9 Privy
10 Ashes
11 Washhouse for
   infected clothes

Service areas
Washhouse areas
Bathrooms
Yard

Figure 47 *The first public washhouse, Upper Frederick Street: (a) plan of the 1842 building [redrawn from plan in James Newland 1856* Report on ... Public Baths and Wash Houses in Liverpool *(Liverpool); (b) the replacement building of 1853; (c) interior view, early 20th century. [Liverpool Record Office, Liverpool Libraries, Photographs and Small Prints]*

Figure 48 *The Paul Street Baths, built in the 1840s following the success of the Upper Frederick Street Baths and Washhouse. It included plunge baths as well as private bathrooms, and again incorporated washhouses and a room for washing infected clothes. [Redrawn from* A Description of the Baths and Wash-houses belonging to the Corporation of Liverpool *(Liverpool: 1846), Liverpool Record Office, Liverpool Libraries]*

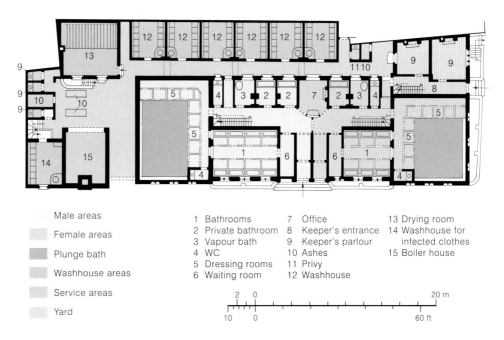

Male areas

Female areas

Plunge bath

Washhouse areas

Service areas

Yard

1 Bathrooms	7 Office	13 Drying room
2 Private bathroom	8 Keeper's entrance	14 Washhouse for
3 Vapour bath	9 Keeper's parlour	infected clothes
4 WC	10 Ashes	15 Boiler house
5 Dressing rooms	11 Privy	
6 Waiting room	12 Washhouse	

Figure 49 *Westminster Road Public Baths, Kirkdale, built in 1876, lacked a washhouse. [Liverpool Record Office, Liverpool Libraries, Photographs and Small Prints]*

time as missing the mark: instead of 'great, pretentious showy structures', some not located where they were most needed, what was required were 'public washhouses conveniently placed ... plain useful buildings'.[17] There were further criticisms that the washhouses were used mainly by commercial washerwomen rather than by householders, but nevertheless these buildings offered an important facility to the poor (at least to the respectable poor). They were imposing buildings externally and highly utilitarian and industrial in character internally. There were no purpose-built washhouses in Kirkdale, but there was a public baths in Westminster Road, built in 1876 (Fig 49), and another in Beacon Street, just to the south, close to the docks and an area of poor housing. The provision of washing sculleries in the improved by-law housing of the late 19th century reduced the importance of public washing facilities, although they continued in use well into the 20th century. The best surviving example is the Steble Street Baths and Washhouse, in the south of the city, opened in 1874 (Figs 50 and 51).

Figure 50 *Steble Street Baths and Washhouse, opened in 1874. The cream brick and lively composition marked the complex out within what was a residential area. [DP039454]*

Figure 51 *An early 20th-century view of the galleried washhouse in Steble Street Baths and Washhouse, showing the washing cubicles, each with a tub and dolly. [Liverpool Record Office, Liverpool Libraries, from Hope 1903]*

Institutions in the suburbs: the landscape of competition

As late as the early 20th century, Liverpool had not eradicated the problem of poor housing and poverty, still highly visible, for those who cared to look, in Vauxhall, Scotland and Netherfield wards immediately to the north of the city centre. Beyond this inner core, however, the achievement had been spectacular. Liverpool's inner ring of working-class suburbs – the former villages of Kirkdale, Walton and Everton in the north, Wavertree and Edge Hill in the east, Toxteth and Dingle in the south – was fully built up by 1900, and the vast majority of the area was filled by terraced housing of the by-law era, providing solid, improved dwellings for those who could afford them. But, although largely a new landscape intended for the respectable working class, it was not without poverty and struggle. These suburban areas were the scene of a battle for the souls of their inhabitants.

Moralists, with some reason, saw the forces of social disruption as represented by the problem of drink. The suburban landscape was astonishingly populated by public houses and other drinking establishments. It was said in 1890 that 'in the south, as in the north, public houses predominate over places of business to a remarkable extent and the majority of them seem to be far more prosperous than the ordinary shopkeepers [sic]'.[18] Over 100 pubs were shown on the 1906 Ordnance Survey map of Kirkdale (*see* Fig 17); Commercial Road, Stanley Road, Kirkdale Road and Walton Road had, in some parts, pubs on one or both sides of the road at virtually every other street intersection (Figs 52, 53 and 54). The numbers suggest that they served a ready market, but not everybody could control their drinking habits. The architectural prominence of some pubs mirrored the views of many social observers on their contribution to poverty.

On the counterbalancing side were the efforts of agencies which had learned the lessons of the recent past. The churches and the local authority were highly visible, the churches from the first development of the suburbs through their construction of places of worship, schools and mission halls, the local authority through its evolving assumption of

responsibility for services such as baths, washhouses, schools and libraries. Charitable institutions also played an important part, moving to provide relief for the poor right in the midst of the community. The emphasis in the suburbs of the late 19th century was, at least as far as institutional buildings were concerned, very much on educating the poor so that they could raise themselves out of their condition. Buildings would suggest that William Rathbone's indirect approach to charitable

Figure 52 (above, left) *Competition for souls: the choice in Stanley Road, with The Knowsley Hotel and, in the background, the Gordon Working Lads Institute.* [DP039600]

Figure 53 (above, right) *Competition for souls: the Mere Bank public house (1881) rivals Everton Library in its decorative façade.* [DP039602]

aid, thrusting the responsibility on to the poor to help themselves, was dominant in the evolution of suburban Liverpool.

Whether out of Christian charity, self-interest or public duty, churches, charitable bodies and local government acted aggressively to improve the moral, spiritual and physical condition of the poor in the hope of producing a fairer, more stable society. The buildings erected for different institutional purposes were, by the late 19th century, not afterthoughts, but were constructed more or less at the same time as the housing erected for the newly established communities. Kirkdale's landscape, like that of Liverpool's other suburbs, was studded with the alternatives to the public house: churches, mission halls, denominational and unsectarian schools, reformatory and industrial schools offering teaching and shelter, reading rooms, libraries and clubs were all present, some challenging the pubs on prominent corner sites, others deeply embedded in the network of humble streets. It was a competitive environment, with sects vying for custom, but no one living in Kirkdale in 1900 could be unaware of the efforts to provide a way out of poverty.

Figure 54 *Competition for souls: the Florrie confronts the Wellie. [DP039449]*

CHAPTER 4

Liverpool: special character, special needs, special places

The institutional character of Liverpool's 19th-century suburbs was little different from that of the suburbs in many other fast developing cities. There were, however, special features of Liverpool's charitable portfolio that either reflected its role as a port or which, if not unique, marked it out from many other places.

The port city

Among the most vulnerable sections of Liverpool society were seamen and their families. Seamen themselves, on shore while their ships awaited cargoes or tides, were regarded as easy prey by the unscrupulous, and the hazardous nature of their trade meant that many suffered injury and required special help. Their families, too, were affected by the death or injury of the breadwinner. Charity came to the rescue of both parties.

The needs of seamen spending time in the port while their ships were in dock were various. So too were the temptations of the dockside area. The spiritual welfare of the sailors was tended by churches dedicated to their use. A floating Mariners' Church, a former merchant ship, was established in 1827 in King's Dock (Fig 55), and much later, in 1883–4,

Figure 55 (right) *The Mariners' Church, moored in the King's Dock: the warship was adapted to give a galleried church to provide services for sailors. It sank in 1872. [Liverpool Record Office, Liverpool Libraries, Photographs and Small Prints]*

Brushmaking: carved panel by John Skeaping on the extension to the Institution for the Blind, Hardman Street (1930–2). [DP039389]

Figure 56 *Gustav Adolfs Kyrka, Park Lane (1883–4, W D Caroe), the Swedish mission church. As well as providing spiritual support to the Scandinavian community in Liverpool, it offered a welfare service to Swedish seafarers, a reading room, and postal facilities. The church still provides support to the Scandinavian community. [DP039563]*

Figure 57 *Church House, Hanover Street (1885, George Enoch Grayson), contained both the Mersey Mission to Seamen and a temperance public house.* [AA047616]

Figure 58 *Opposite Church House is the Gordon Smith Institute for Seamen (1899, James Strong), which contained a library, reading room and meeting hall.* [AA047617]

the Gustav Adolfs Kyrka opened near the docks to provide a place of worship and a reading room for Scandinavian seamen (Fig 56). Respite from the streets was also provided through missions. The Central Institute of the Mersey Mission to Seamen in Hanover Street, built in 1885, offered a recreational refuge and had a chapel and reading rooms: the other half of the building was a temperance public house (Fig 57). Almost opposite, in Paradise Street, was the Gordon Smith Institute for Seamen, and this too offered a place close to the docks where sailors could gather for wholesome recreation (Fig 58).

Safe shelter, however, was also a pressing concern. For those not from the city, a secure billet while on shore was some guarantee against exploitation and a refuge from the easy temptations placed in their path. The streets around the docks were the home of the legendary Maggie May, transported to Australia for a career of robbing sailors, and there were many schemes by which seafarers were relieved of their cash.

Figure 59 *The Sailors' Home, Canning Place, built in 1851 in the style of a Jacobean country house; (left)* exterior *[BB88/00223]; (below)* detail of entrance *[Liverpool Record Office, Liverpool Libraries, Photographs and Small Prints]. On the demolition of the Sailors' Home, the iron gates were removed to Smethwick, Birmingham, where they remain.*

To protect 'Jack Tar' on shore, a hostel was established in Canning Place, close to the docks, in 1844, providing board and lodging at reasonable rates. It soon proved inadequate, however, and new larger premises were opened nearby in 1851. This Sailors' Home, a massive presence, was architecturally extravagant externally; inside, the plain and simple bedrooms opened off an impressive galleried atrium with decorative ironwork (Figs 59 and 60). Nevertheless, temptation was all around: one of the many nearby pubs shown on the mid-19th century Ordnance Survey maps mocked charitable effort with the title of 'The Sailors' Home Vaults'.

Figure 60 *The atrium inside the Sailors' Home: the galleries gave access to cubicle rooms on five floors.* *[BB69/07541]*

Figure 61 (left) *The Royal Liverpool Seamen's Orphan Institution, Newsham Park (1871–5, Alfred Waterhouse). The chapel, which attracted visitors to its Sunday services, has been demolished. [AA047704]*

Figure 62 (right) *The interior of the cavernous and austere dining hall in the Seamen's Orphanage in* c1895. *[Liverpool Record Office, Liverpool Libraries, Photographs and Small Prints]*

Figure 63 (right) *A dormitory in the Seamen's Orphanage in* c1895. *[Liverpool Record Office, Liverpool Libraries, Photographs and Small Prints]*

The hardships caused by injury and consequent loss of livelihood on the part of seamen and their families were mitigated by considerable charitable effort in Liverpool. A Seamen's Hospital was built in 1752 to form a group with the first Infirmary, and its purpose was to provide shelter for 'decayed seamen, their widows and children'. The model for the building was the Royal Hospital for Seamen at Greenwich, begun in 1696, and although it did not compare in scale it was, nevertheless, impressive (*see* Fig 6). In 1771 it housed 413 men, women and children. Later, further refuges were provided for retired sailors: the Liverpool Home for Aged Mariners opened in 1882 in Wallasey, largely funded by William Cliff, merchant, and was made up of cottage homes in a parkland setting, significantly with a view of the shipping on the Mersey.

The problem of sailors' orphaned children was one which created great interest in the mid-19th century, for this group corresponded exactly to the definition of the deserving poor, thrust into moral danger and material want through no fault of their own. Appeals were made to the moral obligation which shipowners especially, and the people of Liverpool more generally, should feel towards the orphans of the sailors who had created their wealth: Lord Derby, opening the huge new Seamen's Orphanage in Newsham Park in 1874, remarked that saving orphaned children 'from the workhouse or the streets is not merely an act of charity; it is an act of duty and of justice'.[19] In a very conspicuous location, the orphanage is the largest building in the area, towering over the park and clearly regarded when built as an ornament to the city (Fig 61). Boys and girls were accommodated (there were just over 300 in 1876), and the complex included playgrounds, a swimming bath, workshops, schoolrooms, dormitories and an immense dining hall (Figs 62 and 63). The orphanage became something of a spectacle, attracting visitors to its chapel on Sundays and acting as a model for how, through discipline, religion and training, charitable effort might result in measurable benefits.

Liverpool was Britain's principal port of embarkation for emigrants to the New World, and this gave the city an opportunity to address the grave problem of destitute and vulnerable children (Fig 64). A scheme for settling children with families in Canada was begun in London, but

Figure 64 *Street urchins awaiting a Christmas feast in St George's Hall. [Liverpool Record Office, Liverpool Libraries, from Birt 1913]*

Figure 65 *The Sheltering Home for Destitute Children, Myrtle Street (1888–9, C O Ellison): this took in destitute children and prepared them for a new life in Canada. [AA047710]*

one of the moving spirits, Mrs Louisa Birt, passing through Liverpool on her way to Canada with a batch of children, was persuaded that the same project could bring benefits here as well. As a result, a sheltering home was established in 1873 and new, larger premises were opened in Myrtle Street in 1889 (Fig 65). Hundreds of children, of widows unable to support them, or of drunkards or violent fathers, were resettled with farming families in Nova Scotia. At Christmas, Mrs Birt, who stayed to preside over the institution, gathered ragged children off the streets and treated them to a dinner, from 1885 held in St George's Hall. The Myrtle Street building, with schoolroom and playground as well as dormitories, survives as a reminder of an extraordinary social experiment.

Helping the disadvantaged and vulnerable

Liverpool's institutional life had a special character derived from the city's maritime function, but it also displayed aspects of charitable provision shared by other towns. Some were a significant presence in the landscape, operating from architecturally important buildings. Liverpool was a pioneer in providing facilities for the blind: for example, its Asylum for the Indigent Blind, founded in 1791, was the first such building in the country. It outgrew its first premises – two converted houses in Commutation Row – and its first purpose-built school, constructed in 1800, was demolished when Lime Street Station was extended. A new

Figure 66 *The Institution for the Blind, Hardman Street (1849–51, A H Holme). The central part provided an entrance hall and shop, the flanking wings (originally single-storeyed) a committee room and female work room. [DP039558]*

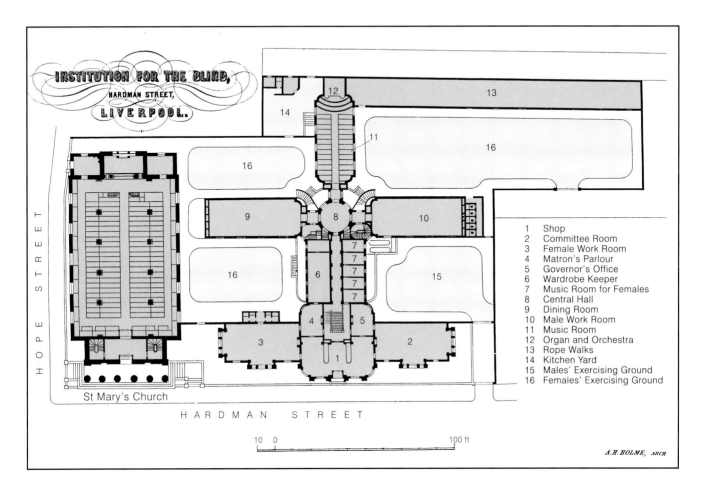

1 Shop
2 Committee Room
3 Female Work Room
4 Matron's Parlour
5 Governor's Office
6 Wardrobe Keeper
7 Music Room for Females
8 Central Hall
9 Dining Room
10 Male Work Room
11 Music Room
12 Organ and Orchestra
13 Rope Walks
14 Kitchen Yard
15 Males' Exercising Ground
16 Females' Exercising Ground

Figure 67 The Institution for the Blind: plan as built, showing the reconstructed chapel removed from London Road. [Redrawn from copy of original published architects' plan kindly provided by Mike Royden]

and larger school was built on Hardman Street in 1849–51 (Fig 66). As well as dormitories, this had work rooms, music rooms, sick rooms and exercising grounds (Fig 67). It also had a shop where items made by the inmates – mats, ropes, baskets – were available for purchase. Further provision was made through the construction of Workshops for the Outdoor Blind in Cornwallis Street (Fig 68). Opened in 1870, this building, in polychrome brick, had workrooms for day visitors, who made baskets, matting and brushes.

The sectarian theme in Liverpool's institutional history cuts into the provision for the blind, for a Roman Catholic Blind Asylum was founded in Islington, near Lime Street, in 1841. The asylum, perhaps better thought of as a school, relocated to the outer fringes of Liverpool in 1899: the new school, in Yew Tree Lane, West Derby (Fig 69), had its own farm supplying milk and vegetables. When the Hardman Street premises of the Institution for the Blind proved too cramped in the early 20th century, it too moved out – at least partially – to the suburbs with the construction of a large new junior school in Wavertree (Fig 70).

Figure 68 *The Workshops for the Outdoor Blind, Cornwallis Street (1870, G T Redmayne), provided employment for the blind. [AA047713]*

Figure 69 *The Catholic Blind Asylum and School, Yew Tree Lane, built in 1899: it had its own small farm, which supplied the asylum with produce. [DP039360]*

Figure 70 *The Royal School for the Blind, Wavertree, built in a spacious suburban setting in 1898–9. [AA047622]*

Figure 71 (left) *The Adult Deaf and Dumb Institute, Princes Road (1886–7, E H Banner), had ground-floor rooms for instruction and recreation, below the first-floor chapel. [AA047619]*

Figure 72 (above) *Memorial glass in the Anglican Cathedral commemorates the work of Josephine Butler in helping the city's prostitutes. [DP039468]*

Figure 73 (above) *Plaque to Josephine Butler in Upper Parliament Street. [DP039568]*

Like the blind, the city's deaf and dumb were provided with special educational facilities. An asylum was established in 1825 and moved to new premises in Oxford Street in 1839–40. Its pupils were either boarders or day pupils, and their education was free. A new and impressive polygonal building on Princes Road was built in 1886–7, and is a distinctive institutional landmark (Fig 71). It has a chapel on the first floor and school rooms below.

Observers of Liverpool's society in the 19th century identified two great problems: drunkenness and prostitution, perhaps only the most visible and, to middle-class sensibilities, offensive aspects of a deep social crisis. There were claims that the two were linked and that both were abetted by connivance on the part of the authorities: one commentator remarked on 'the knitting together of the wholesale liquor trade, of drunkenness, and of prostitution on an enormous scale' and ascribed the prevalence of the evil to 'the power which that interest has obtained within the governing bodies of Liverpool'.[20] The same commentator stated that 443 brothels were known to the police in the late 19th century and that whole districts were effectively turned over to prostitution.

The moral and physical dangers faced by prostitutes were a cause of great concern to social reformers. Josephine Butler, wife of the headmaster of the Collegiate Institution, dedicated herself to improving the lot of women forced into prostitution. She campaigned to change legislation and, on a more local scale, established homes or refuges to provide shelter, instruction and training for employment (Fig 72). Her efforts were matched by those of the different churches, with the result that there were, by the early 20th century, a large number of charities and buildings connected with helping women to escape vice. The Church of England ran the Liverpool Magdalen Home, the Roman Catholic Church offered shelter in the Convent of the Good Shepherd, and perhaps the largest institution was the Female Penitentiary on Falkner Street. Little remains to show how the city responded to the problem of prostitution: a plaque on No. 98 Upper Parliament Street recording the former use of the house as a refuge run by Josephine Butler may be the single reminder of this great charitable effort (Fig 73).

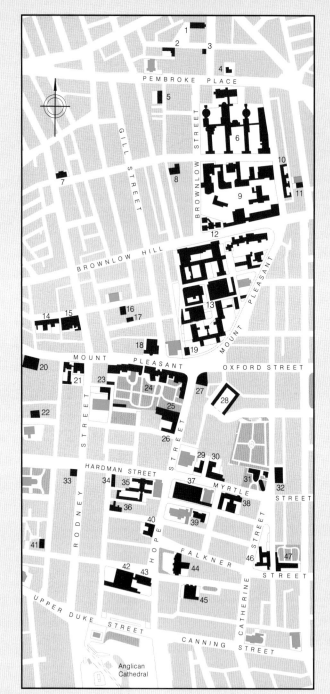

Figure 74 *The institutional quarter: Mosslake Fields in the early 20th century.*
[Reproduced from the 1906 revision Ordnance Survey 25": 1 mile plans,
Lancashire 106.10, 14, supplemented by information from 1890 Ordnance
Survey 10ft:1mile plans.]

Key

1 Daulby Hall, Daulby Street
2 School, Oakes Street
3 Fistula Hospital, Daulby Street
4 Skin Hospital, Pembroke Place
5 Salvation Army Tabernacle, Pembroke Street
6 Royal Infirmary, Pembroke Place
7 St Simon's School, Russell Street
8 County Laboratory, Pembroke Street
9 University College, Brownlow Hill
10 Royal Infirmary, Ashton Street
11 Zion Sunday School, Elizabeth Street
12 Ladies Charity and Lying-in Hospital, Brownlow Hill
13 Liverpool Workhouse, Brownlow Hill
14 School, Pleasant Street
15 Pupil Teachers' College, Clarence Street
16 School, Pleasant Street
17 Latter Day Saints Meeting Room, Bittern Street
18 Wellington Rooms, Mount Pleasant
19 Sunday School, Mount Pleasant
20 Association Lecture Hall, Mount Pleasant
21 Consumption Hospital, Mount Pleasant
22 Caledonian Free School, Oldham Street
23 Church Hall, Rodney Street
24 Convent, inc. Training College and Schools, Mount Pleasant
25 Masonic Hall, Hope Street
26 Roman Catholic Institute, Hope Street
27 Liverpool Medical Institution, Mount Pleasant
28 Almshouses, Cambridge Street
29 Lying-in Hospital, Myrtle Street
30 Eye and Ear Infirmary, Myrtle Street
31 Infirmary for Children, Myrtle Street
32 Infirmary, Myrtle Street
33 Tumour Hospital, Rodney Street
34 Temperance Hall, Hardman Street
35 Institution for the Blind, Hardman Street
36 School, Hope Place
37 Philharmonic Hall, Hope Street
38 Sheltering Home for Destitute Children, Myrtle Street
39 Higher Grade School, Caledonia Street
40 Hahnemann Hospital, Hope Street
41 Mission Room, Knight Street
42 Liverpool Institute (formerly the Mechanics' Institution), Mount Street
43 School of Art, Mount Street
44 Girls' High School, Hope Street
45 Gordon Hall, Blackburne Place
46 Catholic Orphanage for Girls, Catherine Street
47 Female Penitentiary, Falkner Street

■ Institution

■ Place of worship   ▦ Open spaces

0   0.25 km

0   0.25 mile

An institutional landscape: Mosslake Fields

Something of the distribution of local institutions has been demonstrated in the study of Kirkdale, but there also developed a very conspicuous clustering of institutions designed to serve the whole city and the wider region. Mosslake Fields, on the hill above the town, was until the late 18th century open fields, but from that date the area developed as a prestigious residential quarter, first with the fine houses on Rodney Street and later with the construction of terraces and garden squares such as Abercromby Square.

An early presence in the area, however, was the Workhouse, built in around 1770 and expanding from small beginnings to loom large in the landscape. This may have determined the ultimate fate of this part of the city. By the mid-19th century it had been joined by the early components of the Infirmary, and fifty years later three large institutions, all in a line between Pembroke Place and Mount Pleasant, dominated the area (Fig 74). The enlarged Infirmary lay to the north (Fig 75), the fast-growing

Figure 75 (right) *The Royal Infirmary, Pembroke Place (1887–90, Alfred Waterhouse), a striking building: surviving within the former hospital complex are the ward blocks and chapel. [DP039571]*

University College (built with a number of substantial donations from leading merchants and industrialists) occupied much of the central part (Fig 76), and the workhouse had expanded to fill the land between Brownlow Hill and Mount Pleasant. The principal streets in the area were heavily institutional in character: Mount Pleasant was lined on one side with the Young Men's Christian Association (built in 1874–7 in Gothic style), a Consumption Hospital, the Convent of Notre Dame, which

Figure 76 *Victoria Building, Brownlow Hill (1889–92, Alfred Waterhouse), the first major building within the new university, housed administrative offices and the university library. [AA040553]*

included a Training School and College, and the Medical Institution of 1835–7 (Figs 77, 78 and 79). There were further outliers (a Lying-in Hospital and an Eye and Ear Infirmary (Fig 80)), an Infirmary for Children and a large orphanage on Myrtle Street; a homoeopathic hospital on Hope Street; and on Falkner Street was the Female Penitentiary, one of a number of institutions aimed at rescuing women from prostitution. One specialist medical facility stemmed from the city's role as a port with connections across the globe, for a School of Tropical Medicine was

Figure 77 (above) *The YMCA building, Mount Pleasant (1874–7, H H Vale). The ground floor contained a reading room, library and gymnasium, and the first floor had a lecture hall and classrooms. [AA047709]*

Figure 78 (right) *The Consumption Hospital, Mount Pleasant (1903–4, Grayson and Ould), built in red brick and terracotta. [AA047705]*

Figure 79 (right) *The Medical Institution, Mount Pleasant (1835–7, Clark Rampling); the building contained a medical library and a lecture hall as well as committee rooms. [AA040891]*

Figure 80 (left) *Myrtle Street: this view shows part of the Cancer Hospital (1932), the Lying-in Hospital (1861, J D Lee), and the Eye and Ear Infirmary (1878–80, C O Ellison). [DP020632]*

Figure 81 (below) *A later building for the expanded School of Tropical Medicine, Pembroke Place (1913–15, S D Doyle), a link between Liverpool's trading connections with Africa and the merchant wealth generated by this trade. [DP039569]*

founded in the University College in 1898 (Fig 81), largely funded by private donations: the largest came from Alfred Lewis Jones, a hugely wealthy shipping magnate with strong trading interests in West Africa. Finally, there were two further establishments of city-wide importance: the Liverpool Institute, formerly the Mechanics' Institution, comprising a day school for boys on Mount Street and the girls' high school (in Blackburne House) on Hope Street (Fig 82); and the Institution for the Blind (1849–51) on Hardman Street.

In the early 20th century the area as a whole was still mixed in character, with strong survival of the original residential pattern. Later change, however, has consolidated the institutional character of this part of Liverpool and turned it over to education and health, the great growth industries of the 20th century. As wealthy residents moved away (partly perhaps because of the insidious institutionalisation which they saw creeping up the hill) property became available for non-domestic use,

Figure 82 *Blackburne House, Hope Street, a former house converted in 1844 into the Liverpool Institute High School for Girls and extended in the 1870s. [AA047711]*

and the fate of the area was effectively sealed once the Infirmary and the University had settled there. Both expanded greatly from small beginnings and today they form an almost continuous institutional belt stretching well over a kilometre from north to south, interrupted only by the Roman Catholic Cathedral, built on the site of the workhouse. Some of the original charitable institutions have perished or moved away, and many buildings have been converted to new uses. The partial reliance on philanthropy and charity, however, continues to the present day, for some of the most conspicuous modern buildings in this area – the Liverpool Institute for Performing Arts, the Aldham Robarts Learning Resource Centre, the Roy Castle International Centre for Lung Cancer Research (Fig 83) – have benefited from private donations, a well-established expedient applied to contemporary need.

Liverpool's place in the world

Liverpool shares many aspects of its institutional history with other English towns and cities. The responses to the needs of a fast-developing society which it developed in the 18th and 19th centuries are encountered in most cities, in type if not necessarily in scale. Manchester, Liverpool's great partner and rival, provides an interesting comparison. It was advanced in the provision of free public libraries, its main central library opening, like Liverpool's, in 1852, but the construction of free branch libraries outpaced the effort in Liverpool: five existed before 1870. University-standard education also arrived earlier in Manchester, for Owens College was established in 1851 and later formed the cornerstone of the Victoria University, combining colleges in Liverpool, Manchester and Leeds. In other aspects of institutional provision, the two cities marched in step. Manchester's Infirmary of 1752 was established just three years later than Liverpool's, and both cities had a mechanics' institution founded in 1825. The problems of poor living conditions, not significantly less serious in Manchester than in Liverpool, elicited the same response, and its suburbs had a similar range of mission halls, ragged schools and institutes designed to provide a way out of the poverty trap.

Figure 83 *New charitable institutional buildings: the Roy Castle International Centre for Lung Cancer Research, Daulby Street (1997, Franklin Stafford Partnership). [DP039460]*

Where Liverpool differed most significantly from Manchester was in the existence of institutions which sprang from its role as an international port. Its seamen's missions, its sailors' homes, its sailors' orphanage, even the training schools on the hulks in the Mersey, all reflected the special character of Liverpool's function as a trading city. So too did a few institutions which indicate the way in which some parts of Liverpool's society looked out to the world beyond British shores: the School of Tropical Medicine and its associated treatment wards in the Royal Southern Hospital are the most obvious testament to this wider vision. Other great ports show a similar concern for seafarers and their families. Some, flourishing much earlier than Liverpool, also had ancient charitable foundations. Hull, for example, had an endowed grammar school founded in the 14th century and a number of charitable almshouses. Its special association with the sea was evident through charities run by Trinity House, including almshouses for seamen, a Marine Hospital, and schools to train boys for life at sea; and in other institutions such as a seamen's orphanage and a sailors' institute. London, of course, has a long history both of providing for victims of seafaring and of institutions which look out beyond these shores: the London School of Tropical Medicine, for example, was founded just a few months after Liverpool's.

Liverpool's institutional character, then, was formed by two main strands. First, its experience of rapid growth in the 18th and 19th centuries produced a response which can be matched by other cities wrestling with the same problems, although in some cases without Liverpool's enormous trading wealth. And, second, it shows a particular character shared, to a greater or lesser extent, with other ports, for many charitable institutions were devoted to the special needs and outlook of a mercantile city. The institutions of both types were housed in some cases in buildings of great architectural merit, in other cases in structures intended to catch the attention in everyday environments, and in still other cases in simple nondescript structures. Whatever their merits as buildings, however, they all contributed to the city's response to the needs of a varied and rapidly developing society.

CHAPTER 5

Institutions, charity and conservation in the 21st century

The focus of this book has been firmly on the institutional buildings of the 19th century, and the world in which they were built may seem remote to the modern observer. The intervening 20th century transformed the way in which social problems were addressed, with first local government and then the state assuming responsibility for providing services which had been the preserve of charitable institutions. Late in the 20th century, a mixed-economy approach was introduced through the privatisation of some services, principally within the health and education sectors. Today, services are provided by a number of means, with the state in the lead but with private commercial effort and charity still prominent.

Another contrast with the world of 19th-century institutions is the reduction or eradication of the need for particular types of help to the needy. Today most people have ready access to adequate health services, housing and education, and therefore problems of disease, destitution and illiteracy are much reduced from the levels common before 1900. Alternative means are now deployed to meet other needs: institutionalisation is now seen as only one of a number of ways in which help can be administered – large orphanages, for example, are no longer used to cope with the problem of children without parents.

If some needs have diminished, others have grown, and social inequality is as much an issue today as it was in the 19th century. We face challenges in the care of vulnerable groups such as the elderly, asylum seekers and victims of violence, and the work of charitable institutions is of critical importance in the city. There are, perhaps, as many, if not more, charities active in Liverpool today as there were in the 19th century: over 1,200 are registered in the metropolitan district of Liverpool. Many, such as Liverpool Hope University and Nugent Care, generate incomes, and some benefit from substantial donations from modern philanthropists: Bill Gates, of Microsoft, has offered £28 million to fund research and new building at the School of Tropical Medicine; Aldham and Avril Robarts have funded new learning resource centres, both of which received RIBA awards, in Liverpool John Moores University (Figs 84 and 85); and Sir Paul McCartney's financial support has helped to establish the Liverpool Institute for Performing Arts. The

The entrance of the Florence Institute, Mill Street, Toxteth: there are plans to refurbish this important building, derelict for many years, and return it to community use. [DP039581]

new buildings which house these and other institutions are among the most exciting recent additions to the urban landscape.

A number of important points emerge from the study of historic institutions. The first is that there is a strong element of continuity in the use of some buildings. In the centre of Liverpool, the William Brown Library and Museum and the Walker Art Gallery are, perhaps, the best examples of continuity, still providing a focus for the cultural life of the city.

Figure 84 *New charitable institutional buildings: the Aldham Robarts Learning Resource Centre (1992–3, Austin-Smith: Lord LLP), Liverpool John Moores University. [Reproduced by permission of Austin-Smith: Lord LLP]*

The University of Liverpool, too, still uses buildings erected at the end of the 19th century. Away from the central area, the Turner Memorial Homes continue to provide care for the sick, most of the branch libraries still operate, and, in Kirkdale, the Bankhall Girls Institute and the Gordon Working Lads Institute are now youth and community centres, providing important facilities for the area's young people, just as they did when they

Figure 85 *The Avril Robarts Learning Resource Centre (1998, Austin-Smith: Lord LLP), Liverpool John Moores University, Tithe Barn Street. [Reproduced by permission of Austin-Smith: Lord LLP]*

were founded (Fig 86). Many board schools, too, still serve their local communities as they have done for over a century, and their value is being recognised in schemes for retention and refurbishment of some of the best examples of these impressive buildings: modernisation of the most significant part of the Arnot Street Schools complex, for example, will allow it to play a continuing role in primary education.

For some institutional buildings, present uses are closely related to their original function. The Mechanics' Institution in Mount Street, which became the Liverpool Institute High School for Boys, still has an educational use, as part of the Liverpool Institute for Performing Arts. Its former 'sister' school, Blackburne House, (once the Liverpool Institute High School for Girls), is now a centre for women's education and training. In the suburbs, too, institutional buildings have continued to serve their communities in related ways: Steble Street Baths, Toxteth, now functions as a sports centre, and the Congregational community in Orwell Road, Kirkdale, has retreated into the former Sunday school, converting it to a place of worship. In all cases, the new related uses have necessitated adaptation, but change has been accommodated to leave the integrity of the building intact.

Many institutional buildings have been turned to entirely new uses. As the nature of the modern city centre changes, there is considerable pressure to create office space, and many centrally located institutions, such as the seamen's institutes on Paradise Street and Hanover Street, have been converted to commercial use. The popularity of city-centre living has caused other buildings to be converted to residential use: perhaps the largest example is the former Collegiate Institution, Shaw Street (*see* Fig 29). The entertainment industry has taken over other buildings: the Lyceum is now a pub, and, most incongruously perhaps, the Westminster Road Fire and Police Station in Kirkdale recently combined a night club with a kitchen warehouse.

Not all institutional buildings, however, have retained their original use or found a new use which preserves their character. Many have been demolished, a fate that has affected the minor suburban buildings – the mission halls, the ragged schools, even some of the board schools – more than the larger central institutions. Others are underused or entirely unused: some have been empty for a number of years, a perilous situation

Figure 86 *The dedicated team at the Gordon Working Lads Institute, now the Kirkdale Community Centre. [DP039601]*

Figure 87 *Everton Library, St Domingo Road, unused for several years. [DP039346]*

Figure 88 *The campaign to save the Florrie. [DP039451]*

for important historic buildings, the regular maintenance of which is so vital for their future. The most critical cases in Liverpool today are the Seamen's Orphanage in Newsham Park, the Royal Infirmary in Pembroke Place, the Institution for the Blind on Hardman Street, the Wellington Rooms in Mount Pleasant (listed as a Building at Risk on English Heritage's national register), and Everton Library, St Domingo Road (Fig 87). Elsewhere, it is encouraging that schemes are in place which should ensure the future of important historic buildings. The Florence Institute, Mill Street, compromised by years of disuse, was the subject of a vigorous local campaign to save the building, and this has resulted in a substantial grant from the Heritage Lottery Fund, and there is every prospect that it will return to community use in the near future (Fig 88). A new and charitable use has been found for the redundant Roman Catholic Church of St Mary of the Angels, Fox Street, with its adjacent school building: the complex is now used by the Whitechapel

Figure 89 *The Roman Catholic Church of St Mary of the Angels, Fox Street (1910, Pugin and Pugin), with its contemporary school: the complex is now used as a drug rehabilitation centre. [DP039413]*

project, dedicated to drug rehabilitation (Fig 89). It is important that these buildings are kept in use.

The conservation challenge for institutional buildings, whatever their condition or present use, is a familiar one and is about managing the resource in a changing world. Management must be based on an assessment of significance. Collectively, the group must be considered to be of great importance because of the ways in which the buildings demonstrate key aspects of Liverpool's social history. Reduction in the number of buildings making up the group weakens the collective impact of the whole and removes important evidence for the way the city coped with social issues in the period of its greatest growth.

The group is made up, of course, of individual buildings, and it is through these that management of the whole will be effected. Institutional buildings, especially the larger, centrally located ones, figure prominently among the lists of buildings of special architectural or historic interest. The Blue Coat School, School Lane, is listed Grade 1; the Medical Institution, Mount Pleasant, the Collegiate Institution, Shaw Street, the Lyceum, Bold Street, the Wellington Rooms, Mount Pleasant, the William

Brown Library and the Walker Art Gallery are all listed at Grade 2*; and a handful of further buildings are ranked at Grade 2. This gives one measure of significance, both of the group as a whole and of individual structures, but it is an incomplete measure, for the listing criteria militate against the inclusion of buildings dating from after 1850. Most of the city's surviving institutional structures date from the second half of the 19th century, and therefore only the outstanding examples merit inclusion in the list. Many very good buildings are not caught by the listing net, but this should not be taken to mean that they lack importance. The contribution which they make to the local scene and the way in which they represent the social history of the city should be taken into account when weighing whether or not a particular building has significance. The suburban institute, the board school and the public baths all played a central role in the lives of ordinary people, have meaning for the communities which they served, and give a particular identity and character to their areas.

Of course, institutional buildings, like other types, will and must change to adapt to new circumstances. Change can add a new chapter to a building's life and demonstrate that, sensitively handled, these structures can continue to contribute to the life of the city. The outstanding example of new use in an institutional building is the Blue Coat School, School Lane (see Fig 5). For many years this combined an arts venue with retail outlets, and the recent restoration has provided better facilities for these uses in the refurbished building. The key to success in managing change lies in finding suitable uses and in devising design solutions which exploit the character of the building in question. 'Going with the grain' of the building, understanding what it has been used for and how new uses can fit appropriately within its spaces, will help to produce good design and conservation. And good new design alongside a retained historic building can add a dynamic element to the historic environment. Liverpool has important examples of best practice in both these areas.

Refurbishment and conversion to new use are perhaps best seen at the Collegiate Institution on Shaw Street and in Blackburne House, Hope Street. The Collegiate Institution was largely a burned-out shell, so the principal issue on its conversion to residential use concerned the treatment of the external elevations. This was not entirely straightforward, since the new internal spaces did not reflect the fenestration of the main façade, with its large windows extending through two floors. The design solution, by architects Shed KM, retained the tracery of the original building and recessed the new windows within the large openings, a successful compromise which respected the old and provided efficient lighting for the new (Fig 90). In addition, the Collegiate Institution demonstrates a radical solution to the use of the burned-out octagonal assembly hall at the rear of the main range: this has been converted into a garden, and something of the sense of space has been retained in the open area. At Blackburne House, change has been less far-reaching, since the new uses closely match the earlier use as a school, but sensitive handling of the old and interesting and appropriately scaled new features make a satisfying combination.

The Liverpool Institute for Performing Arts provides an excellent example of both the reuse of a historic building (the Mechanics' Institution of 1835–7) and the addition of good modern architecture. The refurbishment of the Mechanics' Institution saw the reinvention of the public auditorium as a theatre, retaining the galleries but using new seating to allow a variety of performance uses (Fig 91). Furthermore, good conservation work on the entrance hall saw the retention of original features to preserve the historic character of the space (Fig 92). A new building, attached on the Mount Street elevation, visually continues the line of the old and employs similar stone facing, but the new is signalled by the curved corner, glazed from ground to eaves (Fig 93).

Quality of design, based on a sympathetic understanding of character, will give a new lease of life to historic institutional buildings. Efforts should be made to find appropriate uses and to think imaginatively about how to exploit the particular qualities which historic buildings display. Brought up to modern standards through careful change, historic buildings offer special environments through the robust, high-quality materials which they employed, and frequently through telling architectural details which bring a building to life. Furthermore, they have associations, for local people and for the local historic

Figure 90 *The Collegiate Institution, Shaw Street: modern glazing has been recessed behind the original mullions and transoms. [DP039412]*

Figure 91 *The Liverpool Institute for Performing Arts (LIPA): the original lecture hall is now used for musical and dramatic performances. [DP039498]*

Figure 92 *The entrance hall at LIPA retains the early cast-iron gates. [DP039497]*

environment. They have generally performed a valuable function for the community for a century or more, so local people understand them as the places where they or their parents were educated or cared for when in need. Bolstering the case for retention of historic institutional buildings is the fact that demolition leaves a gap, both in landscapes and in people's lives. Very often built at the same time as neighbouring buildings, or having been part of the landscape for generations, institutional buildings, even when used for new purposes, form a recognised part of familiar landscapes. Removing them can destroy the integrity of a historic scene, and often results in empty sites which do nothing for the cohesion of landscape or community.

Some buildings will, of course, be lost, for circumstances – economic and social – can preclude the identification of sustainable new uses for redundant buildings. But every effort should be made to find solutions which retain these important buildings. The best examples of conversion and refurbishment demonstrate that they can be landmarks in an area, offer attractive and unique accommodation, and provide a valuable reminder of how agencies such as charities helped to sustain Liverpool in a turbulent period in its history. Just as charitable work continues in new guises in Liverpool today, so too can the buildings of the pioneering period of charitable and institutional provision.

Figure 93 *The modern extension to LIPA (1992–6, Brock Carmichael Associates). [DP039393]*

Notes

1 Troughton 1810, 147, 152

2 Treble 1971, 188

3 *Two Sermons by the Archbishop of York on the Occasion of the Opening of the Chapel at the Liverpool Seamen's Orphanage*, 26–27 September 1874. Liverpool: Gilbert Walmsley 13

4 Lund 1896, 7–8

5 Birt 1913, 109

6 Simey 1992, 131

7 Taylor 1971, 68

8 Miller 1988, 2–3

9 *See* Brown, S and de Figueiredo, P (forthcoming) 2008 for a fuller discussion of the impact of places of worship on Liverpool's landscape.

10 Hope 1903, 89–90

11 *The Porcupine* 8, 30 Mar 1867, 619

12 Grey-Edwards 1906, 86

13 *Liverpool and Merseyside Illustrated*, Nov 1961, 19

14 *Liverpool Citizen*, 7 May 1890, 14

15 *Liverpool Review*, 18 Feb 1888, 11

16 *Speeches on the Laying of the First Stone of the New Mechanics' Institution.* Liverpool 1835

17 *The Porcupine* **16**, 5 Dec 1874, 563–4

18 *Liverpool Citizen*, 18 June 1890, 14

19 Derby 1894, 52

20 Armstrong 1890, 5

References and further reading

Armstrong, R A 1890 *The Deadly Shame of Liverpool: An Appeal to the Municipal Voters*. London and Liverpool

Belchem, J 2000 *Merseypride: Essays in Liverpool Exceptionalism*. Liverpool: Liverpool University Press

Belchem, J (ed) 2006 *Liverpool 800: Culture, Character & History*. Liverpool: Liverpool University Press

Birt, L 1913 *The Children's Home Finder*. London

Brown, S and de Figueiredo, P (forthcoming) 2008 *Religion and Place: Liverpool's Historic Places of Worship*. Swindon: English Heritage

Derby, Edward Henry, Earl of 1894 *Speeches and Addresses by Edward Henry, Earl of Derby*. London

Evans, B 2002 *Mersey Mariners*. Birkenhead: Countyvise

Hope, E W (ed) 1903 *Public Health Congress Handbook*. Liverpool

Lund, T W M 1896 *The Ideal Citizen: An Appreciation of Philip Rathbone*. Liverpool: Howell

Miller, A 1988 *Poverty Deserved? Relieving the Poor in Victorian Liverpool*. Birkenhead: Liver Press

Morris, M and Ashton, J 1997 *The Pool of Life: A Public Health Walk in Liverpool*. Liverpool: Maggi Morris

Owen, D 1965 *English Philanthropy 1660–1960*. London: Oxford University Press

Pollard, R and Pevsner, N 2006 *Lancashire: Liverpool and the South-West*. Newhaven and London: Yale University Press

Royden, M W 1991 *Pioneers and Perseverance: A History of the Royal Liverpool School for the Blind, Liverpool (1771–1991)*. Birkenhead: Countyvise

Sharples, J 2004 *Liverpool*. Pevsner Architectural Guides. New Haven and London: Yale University Press

Simey, M 1992 *Charity Rediscovered: A Study of Philanthropic Effort in Nineteenth-Century Liverpool*. Liverpool: Liverpool University Press. (First published 1951 as *Charitable Effort in Liverpool in the Nineteenth Century*. Liverpool: Liverpool University Press)

Speeches on the Laying of the First Stone of the New Mechanics' Institution. Liverpool 1835

Taylor, I C 1971 'The court and cellar dwelling: the 18th-century origin of the Liverpool slum'. *Trans Hist Soc Lancs and Cheshire*, **122**, 67–90

Treble, J H 1971 'Liverpool working-class housing' *in* Chapman, S D (ed) *The History of Working-Class Housing: A Symposium*. Newton Abbot: David and Charles, 165–220

Troughton, T 1810 *The History of Liverpool*. London and Liverpool